High Performance
with
High Integrity

Publisher's Note:
Memo to the CEO

Authored by leading experts and examining issues of special urgency, the books in the Memo to the CEO series are tailored for today's time-starved executives. Concise, focused, and solutions-oriented, each book explores a critical management challenge and offers authoritative counsel, provocative points of view, and practical insight.

Also available:

Climate Change: What's Your Business Strategy?
Andrew J. Hoffman, University of Michigan
John G. Woody, MMA Renewable Ventures

Five Future Strategies You Need Right Now
George Stalk, the Boston Consulting Group

Manage the Media (Don't Let the Media Manage You)
William J. Holstein, award-winning writer for
the *New York Times*, *Fortune*, and *Barron's*

Lessons from Private Equity Any Company Can Use
Orit Gadiesh and Hugh MacArthur,
Bain & Company, Inc.

High Performance
with
High Integrity

Ben W. Heineman Jr.

Harvard Business Press

Boston, Massachusetts

No part of this publication may be reproduced, stored in or introduced into
a retrieval system, or transmitted, in any form, or by any means (electronic,
mechanical, photocopying, recording, or otherwise), without the prior
permission of the publisher. Requests for permission should be directed to
permissions@hbsp.harvard.edu, or mailed to Permissions, Harvard Business
School Publishing, 60 Harvard Way, Boston, Massachusetts 02163.

Library of Congress Cataloging-in-Publication Data
Heineman, Benjamin W., Jr.
    High performance with high integrity / Ben W. Heineman, Jr.
        p. cm. — (Memo to the CEO)
    Includes bibliographical references.
    ISBN-13: 978-1-4221-2295-2
    1. Business ethics. 2. Organizational effectiveness. 3. Chief executive officers.
4. Boards of directors. 5. Corporate governance. I. Title.
    HF5387.H445 2008
    174'.4—dc22

                                                                2008003057

The paper used in this publication meets the requirements of the American
National Standard for Permanence of Paper for Publications and Documents in
Libraries and Archives Z39.48-1992

Contents

I. The Foundation of the Corporation   1

II. Fusing High Performance
with High Integrity   9

III. Core Principles and Practices   25

IV. The Toughest Issues   100

V. The Right-Sized Role of the Board   147

VI. Building the Foundation   160

Notes   179

Acknowledgments and Dedication   195

About the Author   197

I. The Foundation of the Corporation

In an era characterized by accelerating change, economic dislocation, and—all too often—highly visible scandals, a key question has become more and more pressing. It's a question that is posed not only by the media and by governments, but also in corporate offices around the globe.

What *is* the proper role of business?

This book seeks to provide an answer to that question. Simply put, it argues that contemporary corporations should strive to fuse high performance with high integrity—the twin goals of capitalism.

This calls for some definitions.

- **High performance** means
  - Strong, sustained economic growth
  - That is based on superior products and services, and

- That provides durable benefits both to shareholders and to other stakeholders

- **High integrity** means
  - A tenacious adherence on the part of the corporation to the spirit and the letter of the formal rules, financial and legal
  - Voluntary adoption of global ethical standards that bind the company and its employees to act in its enlightened self-interest
  - Employee commitment to the core values of honesty, candor, fairness, reliability, and trustworthiness—values which infuse the creation and delivery of products and services and which guide internal and external relationships

In the following pages, I explain *why* high performance with high integrity is critically important and why only the CEO can effectively combine them. (See sections II and VI.)

High-performance corporations put relentless financial pressures on their employees to increase net income, cash flow, stock price—pressures that can often cause corruption when unconstrained by high integrity. Meanwhile, the dramatic changes in laws, regulations, stakeholder expectations, and media scrutiny over the past decade can now make a major integrity lapse not just damaging, but devastating. The CEO is fired in disgrace. Billions are squandered through fines, penalties, and lost business. In the worst cases, the company simply implodes.

Combining high performance with high integrity reduces such risks. It can protect the corporation and its stakeholders from catastrophic train wrecks.

But combining high performance with high integrity isn't just about avoiding evils. It also has strong, affirmative benefits for the company: internally, in the marketplace, and in the broader society. Ultimately, it creates the fundamental trust of shareholders, creditors, employees, recruits, customers, suppliers, regulators, communities, and the public at large. Such trust is needed to sustain corporations' enormous power and freedom (even under current regulation): to allocate capital, to hire and fire people, to drive productivity, to invest in new geographies and communities, and to innovate with new products or services.

So this is not a frill or a nice-to-have. It is not the initiative of the month. The fusion of high performance with high integrity is the very foundation of the corporation.

But *how* can CEOs achieve this all-important combination, in the context of a complex global enterprise?

Drawing on my experience of nearly twenty years as a member of GE's senior management team, I seek to answer this question, too. I provide a series of short commentaries that lay out difficult, real-world problems, which I address using eight overriding principles and key related practices (see sections III and IV).

If a CEO wants guidance on some aspect of strategic or financial performance, he or she can find plenty of help in the marketplace. There is literally a flood of books and articles available on those topics. At the same time, there's a smaller—but still respectable—*flow* of books and articles on the subject of business ethics and integrity. But the "performance" literature rarely includes an integrity dimension, and the business-ethics literature tends to put forward general precepts without tackling core organizational realities—without describing how integrity issues must be embedded in business operations, systems, and processes.

This book seeks to bring together both dimensions. I've imagined that I have a morning (and *only* a morning) to brief a CEO and other members of a company's top leadership on fusing performance with integrity. I've tried to avoid both vague generalities and burdensome details, to balance necessary analysis with brief examples, to keep my recommendations practical and realistic. Most importantly, I urge that CEOs move beyond "tone at the top" platitudes and drive a robust performance-with-integrity culture deep into the company: through powerful leadership that voices the vision and the values and through effective management that builds the integrity principles and practices into business operations.

I've also sought to place this discussion in other broad debates about corporations that are going on today in corporate offices and across the globe—and to refocus those controversies:

- **The corporate governance debate.** If we really want to fuse high performance with high integrity, we should focus much more on the "third dimension" of governance—how the CEO actually governs the company—rather than the shareholder–company relationship and director–management relationship.

- **The pay-for-performance debate.** I argue that boards should adopt a new "CEO spec" in succession (and management development) decisions that focuses not just on personal integrity, but also on the individual's capacity and experience to fuse high performance with high integrity. To the same end, they should design compensation systems for CEOs and other top leaders that reward not just "pay for performance," but pay for performance with integrity.

- **The maximize-shareholder-value/corporate-social-responsibility debate.** The basic elements of "corporate citizenship" are high performance and high integrity that recognize the long-term interests of shareholders are advanced by responsibly addressing the concerns of other stakeholders. Those who focus solely on shareholders and those who focus primarily on stakeholders both get it wrong.

- **The "business ethics" debate.** Ethical decisions (e.g., whether or not to commit voluntarily to global standards) don't flow down from abstract morality but grow up from a real-world cost-benefit assessment that includes a company's history, culture, mission, and enlightened self-interest. At the same time, that analysis must recognize that integrity "costs" are investments that deliver benefits over time— benefits that are measured not just by numbers, but also by judgment and common sense.

Because it focuses on these kinds of real-world questions, I hope this book will prove useful not only to CEOs and senior corporate officers, but also to corporate directors, and to those in the media, government, nongovernmental organizations (NGOs), and the public at large who seek to assess whether a given corporation is fulfilling its fundamental obligation to perform with integrity.

Let me add a personal note to this opening section.

These thoughts are drawn from a lifetime of experiences in large public and private institutions. I benefited greatly from conversations with senior leaders in the global business community. I hope the book offers a set of interrelated ideas with wide applicability for enterprises large and small.

But, not surprisingly, I write primarily from the perspective of a senior person at GE, and many of my examples are drawn from that experience. And I write with a distinct sense of humility as just one member of an extraordinarily talented and committed GE team. But I write with humility in another sense too. I don't want to say—or be interpreted as saying—that GE always succeeded. It didn't. We made serious mistakes. We had significant lapses of integrity at the officer level. Not all the ideas here were fully embraced or fully implemented. GE leaders knew the areas for improvement were many. GE's experience only starts an important debate; it hardly ends it.

But I do believe that the senior management of the company cared about these issues. It tried to do the right thing. It devoted serious time, effort, and resources to confronting the performance/integrity challenge across a huge, highly complex, diverse corporation, doing business in more than one hundred nations, with product lines as broad as the world economy, with revenues approaching $200 billion, with net income and cash flow in the $20 billion range, and with employees numbering in the hundreds of thousands. In short, it sought to do things right in a hard-driving, high-performance corporation that took literally thousands of actions with integrity implications every day.

We weren't going to repeal human nature, but we sought to reduce improprieties to a minimum. It was a quest undertaken in good faith, engaging most of the people most of the time, in a very human institution.

II. Fusing High Performance with High Integrity

Global capitalism must candidly face a fundamental problem of integrity: at the very heart of high performance lie fundamental forces that, if left unconstrained, cause corporate corruption.

Top-performing companies apply relentless internal pressure on their people to hit basic financial goals for net income, cash flow, and stock price. Other targets, too, may be critically important: achieving specific returns on investment, equity, or assets; hitting sales or service goals; meeting product development or product launch schedules; and attaining productivity increases, to name a few.

Pressure begets more pressure. "Stretch targets" may put numbers on steroids. The explicit "nice to hit" target becomes an implicit "must do."

Personal incentives are driven by "making the numbers" and therefore create ubiquitous temptations. Employees at all levels may feel that their bonuses and promotions—and perhaps even their job security—depend on falsifying accounts, cutting corners, skipping key process steps, or worse.

Far-flung global enterprises face external pressures, which also create ever-present and illicit temptations. Many non-U.S. markets—from Russia to Brazil, from the Middle East to Asia—suffer from a weak rule of law, endemic corruption, and pervasive conflicts of interest. Yet these same markets are now a critical source of growth for global corporations. Whether that growth is organic or comes through acquisitions, new employees are predominantly local nationals. Not surprisingly, these individuals often come from cultural or business backgrounds that tolerate practices intolerable to a transnational company, such as bribes, shoddy accounting, channeling business to family members.

In most of those nations, moreover, dealing with government is a major element of doing business, because the state defines markets, procures goods and services, taxes income, and makes countless other decisions that decisively affect firm performance. Official extortion and misappropriation are clear and present dangers in places where the rule of law is tenuous, at best.

Local customers, too, may request that companies bend or break rules to facilitate the customers' own private- or public-sector relationships. Similarly, using third-party distribution may be a local or regional necessity, but it tends to raise a host of legal and ethical issues. And with the dramatic enhancement of global supply chains, multinational companies must increasingly worry about the financial, legal, and ethical practices of their sourcing partners.

Unconstrained, these external pressures, too, can corrupt capitalism. And the mix of these external pressures with the firm's own internal pressures can be an especially toxic brew.

The Solution: CEO Fusion of High Performance and High Integrity

At GE, I lived with these pressures and tensions for nearly twenty years. My basic takeaway: I believe that the CEO's core task is to channel the financial pressures properly by fusing high performance with high integrity—in other words, to develop systems, processes, and practices that are built on clearly articulated principles and are based ultimately on a performance-with-integrity culture.

What characterizes this culture? It motivates by values, norms, incentives, penalties, and transparent processes. It doesn't just seek to keep people from misbehaving through threats of discovery and punishment. It also seeks to develop and reward employees who recognize, value, and exemplify integrity. By combining the carrot and the stick, it drives demanding performance built on unyielding integrity, both in small companies and across great global enterprises.

The governance debate of the past ten years has largely missed this fundamental point: only the CEO can affirmatively create the culture and drive fusion of high performance with high integrity. Yes, regulators, outside gatekeepers, and directors all play their important roles, mainly by providing guidelines and checks and balances. But the CEO and senior leadership make it happen.

To understand why this is so, let's revisit some basics briefly. Corporate governance has three dimensions:

- The relationship between the shareholders and the company

- The relationship between the directors and top company leaders

- The relationship between those leaders and the employees

The first bullet point speaks to a core governance issue: what should be the respective powers of the shareholders, the board, and company leaders when it comes to setting commercial strategies and attaining financial performance? Although this is not my main focus, clearly the short-term economic pressures from different types of activist shareholders increase integrity risks.

The second core governance issue delineates the respective roles and responsibilities of company leaders and the board in attaining high performance with high integrity. Fueled by the scandals that increasingly are captured under the umbrella term "Enron," this second governance issue rocketed to prominence at the beginning of this century. Because many of the improprieties of "Enron" flowed from top company leadership—the "Hall of Shame" populated by, among others, Skilling, Fastow, Ebbers, Kozlowski, and Rigas— the focus of many post-Enron reforms has been to increase the roles and responsibilities of the board and its committees in overseeing the CEO.[1]

Indeed, a full-blown governance industry focused on the role of the director has emerged in academia, think tanks, watchdog groups, the investor community, advocacy groups, and the media. (I'm sure that a motivated director could find at least one relevant seminar a week to attend for the rest of his or her corporate life!) Yes, the board has an absolutely critical role to play in choosing, compensating, and evaluating the CEO and other top company leadership.

And yes, it plays an essential role in setting the corporate agenda, identifying the corporation's critical risks and opportunities, and providing advice and oversight regarding those core strategic issues.

Just as important, as I see it, the board needs to create a new spec for CEO selection that includes the desire, ability, and experience to fuse performance with integrity. And finally, the board has to develop CEO compensation plans that don't just "pay for performance," but pay for performance with integrity. (See section V.)

But despite all the scandals, debates, and reforms, one of the most basic facts of life about corporations remains unchanged: the board cannot manage or lead the company. That remains the job of the CEO and the corporation's other top officers. As it turns out, this is especially true when it comes to the foundational task of fusing high performance with high integrity. A board of directors that meets eight or ten times a year simply can't do the heavy lifting—the grinding, complex, day-in, day-out, hands-on work. It's not even a close call: the most pervasive, powerful, and affirmative integrity-related governance issues are the responsibility of the senior leadership, from the CEO on down. How can they drive a demanding performance-with-integrity culture throughout the corporation? The integrity land mines that can blow up in the firm's face are not buried in the corner office; instead they are to be found in all corners of the company.

Many corporations are today seeking to achieve performance with integrity at an operational level. Their CEOs must lead outside, not just inside. They must help shift the center of the public governance debate from its current obsessive focus on board responsibilities to its least discussed and most important dimension: governance on the front lines.

The Benefits of Avoiding Risk: New Realities

In a rapidly changing world, one fundamental benefit of fusing high performance with high integrity is reducing unwanted risk and cost—avoiding the kind of major integrity misstep that would have catastrophic consequences for a corporation.

I was at GE from 1987 to 2005. In roughly that same period, and particularly in this decade, there was a sea change in legal and regulatory trends in the United States—and, increasingly, around the world. Previously, the CEO who paraded a confident leadership style and accelerated financial results won widespread trust and admiration. Not so today! For a whole host of reasons ranging from scandals to globalization, the world is a much more skeptical, critical, and adversarial place.

Consider, for example, the "legalization" of accounting rules in the wake of the financial-engineering scandals. Of course, outright fraud or reckless accounting actions should be punished. But good-faith accounting interpretations that several decades back would have been the subject of a conversation with the office of the SEC's chief accountant are now the focus of an informal (or formal) inquiry from the SEC's beefed-up enforcement division—and may result in negotiated consent decrees.[2]

This is symbolic of broader regulatory trends. A decade ago, regulators would usually create new rules, or clarify ambiguous ones, through administrative rule making. This process sought broad input from the regulated and other affected parties, and had a prospective effect: nobody looked backward. Today, impatient regulators try to change the law through enforcement cases against individual companies—and are inclined to impose legal sanctions retroactively for past corporate actions taken in good faith but now judged "improper" under changing expectations or standards.

By any measure, this is a big change. The Justice Department and other federal regulatory agencies, seeking to criminalize regulatory statutes, jockey for position with state attorneys general. Meanwhile, in addition to enhanced government enforcement across a range of traditional issues—topics like antitrust, anti-bribery, and securities law—regulators are expanding enforcement on newer issues like privacy, consumer protection, money laundering, and export licensing. At the same time, enforcement is burgeoning else-where, in both the developed and the developing worlds.[3] Finally, with trust eroded by scandal, the media—encouraged by a dramatic rise in watchdog groups and other nongovernmental organizations—today make any consequential corporate failing front-page or 24/7 news.

Debates can rage about whether or not all these policy and media shifts are a "good" thing. But they exist, and they pose accelerating threats to the eco-nomic health and reputation of corporations.[4]

Any business leader who has been through an in-tense government investigation—and I am certainly one—can testify to its huge and negative impact. Enormous amounts of time, effort, and treasure are consumed. Key executives come to view each other with distrust. The CEO and other leaders get dis-tracted, spending weeks and even months ensuring that the company's response is complete and correct. Typically, problems compound themselves, as other regulators and private litigants, not just in the United States but sometimes in different nations, launch parallel proceedings. Suddenly, the company faces a three-, four-, or five-front war.

What happens when there is not just smoke, but also fire? The corporate consequences can range from significant to dire. In the wake of egregious integrity violations, companies may be forced into bankruptcy, or even collapse. The hit to the bottom line can be enormous. As recently as a decade ago, a fine or penalty or settlement in the $100 million to $200 million range was considered large; today, comparable events can reach into the billions.

The individual consequences, too, range from the humiliating to the catastrophic. In the last decade, the media has reported that many once celebrated CEOs have lost their jobs (or left ahead of schedule) due, in whole or in significant part, to company integrity issues: Hank Greenberg at AIG (company accounting), Frank Raines at Fannie Mae (company accounting), Peter Dolan at Bristol-Myers Squibb (failure to inform the board), Phil Condit (procurement scandals) and Henry Stonecipher (employee relationship) at Boeing, John Browne at BP (safety practices), and Klaus Kleinfeld at Siemens (widespread improper payments), among others. Others, including those Hall of Shame members mentioned earlier, have, of course, received stiff jail sentences and been hit with large financial fines and penalties.

But other consequences growing out of a major integrity lapse can have an even greater long-term impact. Business relationships are put through the grinder. A corporate reputation built over years or decades gets shredded overnight. The market cap tanks. Eventually, if the damage is deep enough, all stakeholders are hurt. Employees lose their jobs, retirees lose their pensions, shareholders lose their equity value, creditors eat bad debts, customers lose a supplier, suppliers lose a buyer, and communities suffer in a variety of ways from lost or reduced business.

The next thing that happens, not surprisingly, is that a cry goes up for new laws and regulations to keep this from ever happening again. Corporate efforts at self-policing are ignored, mainly because they appear belated, half-hearted, or hypocritical. Suddenly, the policy-making apparatus lurches forward, often with uncertain or undesirable results.

My main point is that the CEO's job today is far different than it was twenty or even ten years ago. The changes have come from almost every direction: in the form of laws, regulation, enforcement, stakeholder activism, stakeholder expectations, and media scrutiny, to name just a few. As a result, business leaders today must work much harder, and more effectively, to navigate the shoals of a more hostile, less forgiving environment—even as they attempt to succeed in a hypercompetitive global economy.

The lesson seems clear. To avoid unwanted risk and cost for their companies, their stakeholders, and themselves, today's CEOs must fuse high performance with high integrity.

The Affirmative Benefits of Corporate Citizenship

So far, I've accentuated the negative. But fusing high performance with high integrity also fosters "corporate citizenship," which—when properly conceived— creates affirmative corporate benefits: inside the company, in the marketplace, and in the broader society.

As I define it, corporate citizenship has three interrelated elements:

- Strong and sustained economic performance

- Robust and unwavering adherence to the spirit and letter of the relevant financial and legal rules

- The establishment of, and adherence to, binding global standards—extending beyond the requirements of formal rules—that are in

> the company's enlightened self-interest
> because they promote its core values, enhance
> its reputation, and advance its long-term
> economic health

And these elements are all made possible by employees committed to the values of honesty, candor, fairness, reliability and trustworthiness.

Corporate citizenship, so defined, is a far more useful framework for assessing the appropriate role of business in society than the erstwhile lens of "corporate social responsibility" (CSR), which, by its terms, ignores core economic performance. Corporate citizenship more accurately reflects the corporation's actual interdependent relationships with its various stakeholders—employees, pensioners, shareholders, creditors, customers, end users, suppliers, communities, and regulators—upon which its performance depends.

It also avoids a tunnel-vision focus on increasing shareholder value, usually in the short term. This simplistic value-maximization theory—which holds that the corporation is merely the agent of its stockholders—is reflected neither in corporate law nor in practice.[5] In the 1920s, that decade of commercial excess, GE's highly respected CEO Owen D. Young acknowledged that the company owed its shareholders a fair rate of return—but went on to say that it also bore an obligation to labor, customers, and the public so that it could behave "as a great and good citizen should." This broad-gauge philosophy has been embraced by many CEOs since.[6]

Having participated in more CSR discussions than I can count, I can state with confidence that the first element of corporate citizenship—strong and sustained economic performance—is all too often ignored or downplayed by the advocates of CSR. At the same time, surprisingly, it is not forcefully articulated by CEOs. Let me use GE as an example.

Today, GE has more than 5 million shareholders, many of whom are retirees. It distributes about half its profits—that is, more than $8 billion annually—in dividends. Over the years, it has done business in a way that has caused a steady appreciation in its stock price.

The company sustains (or helps sustain) more than three hundred thousand employees, as well as their more than seven hundred thousand family members. It ensures retirement payments for more than six hundred thousand present and future pensioners. It seeks to provide high-quality goods and services to hundreds of millions of customers around the world.[7] Every year, it buys more than $50 billion in materials, components, goods, and services, with huge multiplier effects. Its strong performance, moreover, has been sustained over many decades. And like many companies today, it seeks to grow its businesses profitably by addressing some of society's most pressing issues. One example among many is the company's ecomagination initiative, aimed at providing technologies to reduce its customers' greenhouse gases.

High integrity—the adherence to formal requirements and the voluntary commitment to ethical standards and values—yields many affirmative benefits. Inside the company, it helps attract and retain top talent. It empowers employees to speak up on both performance and integrity concerns. It contributes mightily to meritocratic employment practices. It helps create a culture of alignment between personal values and company values, thus improving morale, pride in the company, and productivity.

In the marketplace, it enhances the brand, contributes to the integrity of products and services, differentiates the corporation from its competitors, minimizes customer complaints, and addresses investor concerns. By so doing, it advances company growth.

In the broader society, it enhances the company's reputation, which in turn provides credibility in public policy debates; enables respectful relationships with regulators; generates positive media, which in turn augments brand and reputation; provides a positive example in "integrity-challenged" emerging markets; and helps generate trust for "business" writ large.

So, avoiding devastating risk and achieving affirmative benefits in the company, the marketplace, and society is *why* the CEO must lead in fusing high performance with high integrity. In the next two sections, focusing on core principles, key practices, and tough issues, I turn to *how* he or she can do it.

III. Core Principles and Practices

The key to achieving sustained high performance with high integrity lies in creating the right CEO-led corporate culture—the shared principles (values, policies, and attitudes) and the shared practices (norms, systems, and processes) that influence how people think, and therefore how they behave.[1]

What are the constraints on the internal and external pressures to make the numbers which can lead to corruption? One answer is a disciplinary culture: people are afraid of violating company precepts (or breaking the law!), getting caught, and being punished. But there's a positive answer, as well. In a robust performance-with-integrity culture, affirmative values and norms of behavior are so widely shared that people want to win the *right* way. Such a culture is created as much by aspirations, examples, transparency, and incentives as it is by penalties.

When I gave performance-with-integrity presentations to GE business leaders, I leaned heavily on a slide that had only two bullets:

- Create the systems and processes

- Create the culture

The two are complementary, and inseparable. Company leaders create a culture by forcefully and consistently articulating the organization's code of conduct, guiding principles and policy standards—in speeches and in written communications. At the same time, though, the company has to implement a robust set of practices that:

- Track business disciplines

- Have real consequences

- Use needed resources

Setting a verbal "tone at the top," without such effort, is just window dressing.

During my time at GE, the company sought to pursue performance with integrity with characteristic business rigor: setting goals, building systems, running disciplined processes, defining meaningful measurements, and auditing systematically. At the same time, we were well aware that creating a high-performance-with-high-integrity company is truly a journey without end, because corporations simply can't abolish fraud and corruption. Inevitably, they will encounter internal wrongdoing—and they will learn, as GE did, hard lessons from integrity violations that went on too long and involved too many.

In a transnational company, moreover, the high-performance-with-high-integrity culture must be strong and unyielding everywhere in the world. The core principles and practices that create that culture, therefore, also must be uniform and universal across different business lines, different markets, and different regions. True, the transnational company must always be sensitive to local conditions. But variation on these fundamental cultural issues is hypocritical and confuses people. It is antithetical to integrity. It risks creating a cancer that can metastasize across the company, eating away at the culture.

A salient example: A catastrophic explosion at a BP plant in Texas killed fifteen people and injured two hundred more. It sparked civil and criminal proceedings, and led, ultimately, to criminal pleas and fines. An independent panel established by the BP board and chaired by James Baker concluded that, "BP has not provided effective process safety leadership and has not effectively established process safety as a core value across all five of its U.S. refineries." This Baker Panel conclusion, and its other criticisms of BP culture, was reported by the media to be an important factor in iconic CEO John Browne advancing his planned retirement date by more than a year.[2] In creating and supporting a high-performance-with-high-integrity culture, CEOs must focus on those first-order issues where leverage is greatest. Drawing from my own experience and observations, I believe there are eight interrelated principles, and key implementing practices, that are fundamental, and nonnegotiable. They constitute the rest of this section.

Principle 1: Demonstrate Committed and Consistent Leadership

An unequivocal and unyielding leadership commitment is the beginning—and also the end—of creating a performance-with-integrity culture.

This commitment is only understood *and* felt by the company when there is a seamless consistency between leaders' personal attributes, their public and private statements, and their direct and indirect actions. High standards for employees demand high standards from senior leaders. Let me highlight six imperatives.

1. Leaders Must Lead

This sounds obvious, but it's not. GE often confronted a misperception that turns out to be endemic at many corporations: the notion that business leaders must focus on business—sales, marketing, new products, pricing, deals, and the numbers—and that the staff (primarily finance, legal, and human resources) owns the responsibility for integrity systems and processes.

"I just don't have the *time*," was the typical business leader's lament. The most important step a CEO can take is to reject that assertion—publicly and vehemently—and to make clear to the organization that the leaders at all levels of the corporation share the responsibility (along with the CEO) for communicating values and implementing related practices. Yes, staff officers play a vital, complementary role on integrity issues. But there is no chance of fusing high performance with high integrity unless all executives understand that this is their most fundamental leadership task. It is the yardstick they must use as they hire people, build their organizations, set priorities, and allocate resources—and by which they will be held accountable.

2. Put Integrity First

Most companies have a short mission statement that commits the organization to broad goals like innovation, customer satisfaction, growth, or specific personal traits (e.g., edge, energy, execution). One can debate whether these mission statements have any significant impact, in and of themselves, but it is surely a glaring omission if the CEO does not make "integrity" the foundation value upon which all others rest. CEOs must also make written corporate codes of conduct a core, personal message.

But the fundamental point is best delivered in person, in clear and unmistakable terms. At GE, Jack Welch (and later Jeff Immelt) put special emphasis on two annual agenda-setting meetings of senior executives: the first consisting of the company's 220 officers in October, and the second comprising the company's 600 senior executives (including the officers) in January. Welch (and subsequently Immelt) opened and closed each and every one of these meetings with strong statements about performance with integrity, centering on four main points:

- GE is built on our reputation as a world-class company. Our performance with integrity is the foundation of that reputation. That reputation is of tremendous benefit.

- Each senior leader in this room is personally accountable for the integrity of the company—it is the primary responsibility of GE business leaders. This means establishing the right systems and processes, and creating the right culture.

- No cutting of corners for commercial considerations will be tolerated. Integrity must never be compromised to make the numbers.

- For those in this room—those to whom the rest of the company looks for guidance—one strike and you're out. You can miss the numbers and survive; you cannot survive when you miss on integrity.

Obviously, the company's senior leaders took many lessons from these high-level meetings back to their respective businesses (spread to all employees in later years via webcasts)—but this key CEO message was always prologue and epilogue to the year's business narrative that was retold across the company.

3. Go Beyond "Tone at the Top"

The way chief executives exercise moral judgment is much more important than company policy.[3] Specifically, the CEO must make it clear that the top executives of the corporation will not be spared nor favored, but will be held every bit as accountable for lapses in integrity as they are for other performance failures—and that in fact, the "generals" will be held to even higher standards than the "troops."

To cite a case in point, a seasoned GE business leader—operating in an emerging market under competitive pressures—willfully sidestepped the company's due diligence procedures when shifting distribution from employees to a third party. An internal audit subsequently revealed serious misbehavior by that third party. The upshot? The distribution arrangement was terminated, and the officer was compelled to resign, even though he was very "successful" in a highly competitive market. There was no equivocation, or rationalization, or protracted weighing of the pros and cons. The executive had crossed a line that leaders should defend, not bend. The tough words delivered at senior leader meetings—competitive pressures never justify compromising integrity, and "one strike and you're out"—were driven home by tough action.

An even more powerful—indeed a thunderous—message is sent through the removal of senior executives whose failure is one of omission, rather than commission. Most often, this involves situations in which improper acts within a business unit go undisclosed and unreported for too long or involve too many people—all powerful indicators of a cultural failure.

One example was uncovered in the early '90s, while Jack Welch was CEO; a second surfaced a decade later, early in Jeff Immelt's tenure. The former involved a fraud against the U.S. government in an Israeli Air Force jet fighter procurement financed by U.S. funds. The latter involved a Japanese customer who insisted that GE employees falsify documents relating to safety issues; these documents, in turn, were submitted by the customer to in-country regulators.

Both matters grew out of the dark side of customer satisfaction. Both were understood to be wrong by many in the organization. Both involved many individuals who either engaged in improper conduct themselves or failed to have it investigated or stopped.

Both precipitated the most important CEO integrity decisions during my time at GE. The company had to root out the facts rigorously, work closely with the governments involved, effect fundamental changes in certain systems (e.g., better education, better process checks), and discipline many lower-level employees. But the most painful and difficult actions involved the senior officers who led the business units. They had had long careers with the company and were widely regarded as "good guys" by other senior leaders. They had no personal knowledge of the bad acts. But they had failed, in a most dramatic way, to create a performance-with-integrity culture. Far too many in their organizations were indifferent to intolerable acts for far too long.

The executives were asked to leave the company. The message was clear: there is no favoritism. The

CEO holds top leaders to high standards, and those who are indifferent to creating an integrity culture will be gone.

4. *Communicate Decisions Candidly*

The CEO gets the most impact out of disciplining senior executives when those actions are discussed candidly with top leadership. In both the Israel and Japan episodes described above, the CEO (first Welch, then Immelt) asked me to describe in detail to the six hundred executives at the January goal-setting meeting exactly what had happened and why they had asked the officers involved to leave the company. In each case, my presentation lasted fifteen minutes. Never before or since have I spoken to audiences so large that were so silent—and motionless. Both Welch and Immelt drew upon my presentations in their closing remarks, driving home the point that *sustained* negligence in creating a performance-with-integrity culture is grounds for dismissal.

Let me hasten to say that delivering a positive message to the top leadership group is equally effective. Shortly after becoming CEO in 2001, Jeff Immelt instituted Chairman's Leadership Awards at the January meetings of the six hundred senior executives. The awards recognized top performers from the prior year. Some awards go to the business unit with the best overall performance, or the person who developed a great new product, or the business with the terrific productivity increases. But other awards go to the internal audit staff, or to a successful environmental program, or to a person who has made a contribution to governance—and this speaks volumes to company leaders about the core value of high performance with high integrity.

5. Leaders Must Embody Values

Companies are exquisitely attuned to hypocrisy on the part of their leaders. The CEO delivers a stirring call for "performance with integrity!" at a large company meeting but then—at some smaller meeting—makes a cynical comment that points in the opposite direction. That second comment, too, flashes out across the organization, relayed, amplified, even distorted, by word of mouth. Similarly, CEO winks and nods that sanction improprieties, personal actions (dishonesty, lack of candor) that contradict bedrock company values, and the disparagement of officials who raise integrity questions about corporate action—all erode credibility and commitment.

We don't need, and won't get, saints in our corner offices. When huddled with the small core of senior managers who deal with them every day, CEOs may be earthy, frustrated, skeptical, cynical, angry, volatile. But for employees who do not see the CEOs every day, loose language from the top is confusing (at best), and CEO cynicism or winks and nods are deadly.

In other words, for CEOs, nearly every employee event is a "public" meeting, demanding personal behavior that is consistent with company values.

6. Senior Executives Must Be
Both Leaders and Managers

CEO commitment and consistency—and all the other principles and practices that follow below—require both the leadership and management skills that John Kotter described almost two decades ago.[4] Management is about coping with complexity in a large organization, through the disciplines of planning, goal setting, organizing, staffing, budgeting, and auditing. Leadership is about coping with change, and expressing the powerful aspiration of fusing performance with integrity when markets, enforcement, and public pressures are in constant motion. It is also about inspiring and energizing people—not just by pushing them in specific directions through controls, but by articulating a vision, and satisfying the basic human need to belong in a strong culture that lets them live up to their ideals.[5]

Principle 2: Manage Performance with Integrity as a Business Process

The hardest aspect of fusing high performance with high integrity is getting business leaders to invest the time and effort needed to embed key integrity principles and practices into business processes. In other words, the CEO must get them to embrace performance with integrity when they are wearing their "manager's hat." Again, I highlight six practices that can help make this difficult job easier.

1. Confront Complexity

All companies struggle with a fundamental challenge: the vast array of financial and legal rules that apply to their every activity. These rules are voluminous, multifaceted, ambiguous in interpretation, and uncertain in application. I was, frankly, stunned when I began my tenure at GE in 1987 and began to get a sense of the complexity that the company faced.

In the United States alone, companies must deal with a myriad of rules and regulations of general effect (for example, promoting fair markets, protecting social goods, or giving rights to stakeholders) as well as specific rules applying to particular industries (aviation, energy, communications, etc.). These rules are often highly complex. (FAS 133, regulating derivatives, is literally hundreds of pages long.) They may be ambiguous and therefore hard to interpret. The rules at the federal, state, and local levels may overlap, or even contradict each other.

These problems of complexity, ambiguity, uncertainty, and mutual inconsistency are multiplied a hundredfold for a transnational company like GE, which is subject not only to international law, but also to the laws of more than one hundred nations. Among these foreign regulatory regimes, a company can encounter serious conflicts between the central and local authorities (e.g., in the EU or in China); or episodic, erratic, or corrupt enforcement (emerging markets); or fundamentally different legal systems (common law versus civil law versus Islamic law). And to complicate matters still further, different employees have widely varying obligations, depending on their level, function, industry, market, or nation.[6]

It all adds up to enormous complexity, in a realm where many issues come in gray, rather than black and white, and in which considerable judgment may be required. Nevertheless, complexity must be confronted and overcome. And until a given rule or regulation is changed (in aboveboard and legal ways), it needs to be followed.

2. Build the Integrity Infrastructure

The CEO's response to this complexity starts with building the integrity infrastructure: developing rigorous systems and processes to prevent, detect, and respond. At GE, the shorthand for this task was to establish an integrity program across each GE segment that:

- Prevents ethics and compliance misses . . . and when prevention fails . . .

- Detects misses as soon as possible . . . and once they are detected . . .

- Responds quickly and effectively

In other words, the job is building an "integrity factory," which is hard work. The writing on this topic for company staff functions is voluminous, but here are the essentials.[7]

Prevention. The first critical step in prevention is risk assessment. This involves taking an inventory of the important financial and legal rules in all product lines and in all places where the corporation does business. The company must then review its different business processes for all those products and locales, and makes decisions about which activities are high risk. Risk arises from such factors as the complexity of the applicable rules, current trends in enforcement, newly hired or acquired employees, the impact of a miss, or difficult geographies.

The second critical prevention step is risk abatement or mitigation. In general, this means building information tracking and control processes in all business functions (e.g., sales, marketing, manufacturing, engineering, M&A, sourcing) for key risks. Company specialists need to develop customized tools—like acquisition-integration templates for deal teams or a digitized system for tracking environmental issues for plant managers—so employees in high-risk positions can handle complex general tasks and address sensitive issues like improper payments or conflicts of interest.[8]

One technique that GE has tried for risk assessment and abatement involves making a senior business leader in each major business division the "champion" for a particular policy area—for example, labor and employment, export controls, antibribery—and teaming him or her with a substantive specialist in those fields. (These experts may come from the business unit, from corporate headquarters, or from outside the company.) This team then assesses the risks associated with different business processes: manufacturing, engineering, research and development, facilities management. Business leader involvement at this early risk-assessment / risk-abatement stage leads to better operational responses and also sends a strong message to the organization.

Recently, for example, top leaders at GE Aircraft Engines took on 14 key policy areas, identified 56 risk areas, and conducted 328 assessments across 14 different functions and P&Ls to focus on high-risk subjects such as export control laws, information security, FAA quality controls, product safety, and controllership.

Detection. By the time a company learns of an SEC or Justice Department investigation, or an inquiry from a consumer-protection authority in Europe, it's late in the game—often very late. The corporation is on the defensive and has lost some control over the issue. Far better to uncover the bad news first and deal with it!

Robust internal systems for detecting possible improprieties as soon as possible give the corporation time to determine the facts, decide whether the issue needs to be reported to the authorities, and pinpoint perilous weaknesses in the integrity infrastructure that need immediate attention. Of course, general management oversight and control processes help surface questions about integrity issues. But giving employees voice—through an ombuds system or other means—is also critical to detection. It's so important to performance with integrity, in fact, that I address it below as a stand-alone principle.

Response. Responding to concerns about possible improprieties has four basic dimensions:

- Investigation

- Individual discipline

- Remediation within the business unit

- Remediation across the company, when appropriate

Internal inquiries must be pursued fully and fairly— usually by the financial, audit, and legal staffs—with no potential for "waive-off" if the inquiry moves higher up into the company. When deciding upon appropriate disciplinary actions, the business unit should draw on the broad experience of corporate leaders: the chief financial officer (CFO), the general counsel (GC), the HR leader and—in very important and difficult cases—the CEO. (Jack Welch and Jeff Immelt spent extraordinary amounts of time working through difficult disciplinary cases.) What has the company done in similar cases in the past, with respect to monetary penalties (reduced salary, bonus, or equity grant) or career impact (demotion, delaying a promotion, termination)?

At times, the impropriety—such as cheating on an expense account—simply grows out of a personal weakness. But much more often, the poor behavior is made possible by poor risk assessment and poor risk mitigation—in other words, bad systems and processes. So root-cause analysis and system improvements are almost always an essential step, after the individual involved has been disciplined.

At one point, we uncovered an embezzling scheme at a remote site in GE's financial-services business in Thailand. An "after-action" investigation revealed systemic problems at remote sites—not just in financial services, but in other business as well, not just in Thailand, but elsewhere. This was a GE-wide problem, requiring a GE-wide solution.

3. Merge Business and Integrity Processes

It is the ultimate responsibility of the P&L leadership teams to embed the essential elements of the integrity infrastructure into all the business processes: from small units to large divisions, from manufacturing and engineering to marketing and sales, from sourcing and information technology to M&A and R&D. This means integrating relevant abatement mechanisms into *each* basic operation. Sales teams, for example, are affected by competition laws, prohibitions against improper payments, and rules against false product claims. Risk mitigation processes for these (and other) issues must be built into sales processes—not just used as fodder for lectures to the sales team once a year.

Similarly, this merger of business and integrity processes must occur not just across multiple risks in multiple operations, but also across multiple regions. Once this "integrity factory" has been built—and auditing and evaluation processes are in place—then the framework for high performance with high integrity exists.

As an example, GE sought to drive environmental, health, and safety issues deep into manufacturing, thereby making the plant managers and manufacturing leaders responsible for those issues, and the P&L leader ultimately accountable. Quarterly reports on each facility in each business on key parameters (spills, accident rates, notices of violation) were rolled up into a master matrix, and these cross-business comparisons were sent to the CEO. As one can imagine, landing in the bottom quartile pro-

vided the relevant business leaders with strong incentives for improvement![9]

4. Deploy "A" Players—
and Adequate Resources

In most corporations, there is a constant struggle to
find the right people and allocate adequate resources.
Unless both happen, though, the merger of integrity
and business processes can't happen.

Hiring "A" experts on company-critical areas of financial and legal regulation inside the corporation is
vital—and cost-effective—for risk assessment and abatement. The advantage of the inside experts is that
they learn the company far better than any outsider,
and they can act quickly, rather than calling outside
for help. For example, Jack Welch encouraged me to
hire an outstanding expert in taxes (John Samuels)
and another in environmental programs (Steve Ramsey) who had developed world-class expertise both in
government service and in private practice. Beyond
minimizing and mitigating integrity risks, they also
proved extremely valuable to the CEO in transactions and financial planning, and in both offensive
and defensive public policy. Bringing outside experts
inside goes against the grain in many companies, but
it often proves well worth the effort.

Questions about paying for the integrity infra-structure also need to be faced candidly and system-atically. There's no way around it: funds must be found and spent to establish the fundamentals. Un-less the CEO makes dedication of adequate re-sources a clear performance metric for business leaders, these costs inevitably get shoved to the bot-tom of the list. This is a forward commitment, as well: when the company engages in the next round of "10 percent across-the-board cost cuts," the CEO and other business leaders must fight the temptation to wield the meat ax in the name of administrative simplicity in this sensitive area, and scrutinize the ac-tual impact of reductions. This struggle arose almost every year that I was at GE, and I have no doubt that our experience was typical. According to a govern-ment report, cost cutting of maintenance and up-keep, without due regard to safety impact, was one cause of BP's catastrophic Texas plant explosion (a conclusion BP disputes).[10]

To be sure, particular performance-with-integrity processes should be evaluated for efficacy and effi-ciency as part of the continuous drive for produc-tivity. In fact, simplification and quality disciplines can improve both performance *and* integrity—for example, when Six Sigma manufacturing at the front end reduces pollution abatement costs at the back end.

5. Make "Management Integrity Reviews" Real Events

Management integrity reviews are evaluations that business leaders use to drive accountability in their respective units, and that are subsequently used to drive accountability across the company.

At GE, the business division leaders (e.g., Energy, Aircraft Engines, Healthcare, Consumer Finance) are responsible for separate, regular reviews of their adherence to controllership precepts, to legal and ethical rules, and to environmental health and safety requirements.[11] Each focuses on risks, abatement, and results, as well as on controversies that raise systemic integrity issues. Each business reports integrity metrics, which are compared year over year.[12] Some businesses have developed a best practice by merging integrity metrics with performance metrics and representing the results on the digital dashboards now used for continuous business assessments.

At the company level, the corporate audit staff independently reviews businesses performance-with-integrity processes on a near-continuous basis. The CEO personally reviews business financials six times a year. The companywide policy compliance review board (comprising the CFO, GC, HR leader, head of the internal audit staff, and senior prevention officer) reviews each major business annually, receives integrity report-outs three times a year from the corporate audit staff, and assesses major cases and investigations on an "as needed" basis. This board annually assesses the company's compliance programs, major risk areas, need for new initiatives, and adequacy of resources. Cross-company councils—financial, controllership, legal—also meet regularly to share best practices and address emerging issues systematically, from a specialist perspective. Finally, corporate leaders in tough, unique markets—like China, the Middle East, or Russia—also conduct cross-business financial and compliance reviews to share problems, best practices, and region-specific strategies.

As with many other business issues, the process of preparing for the reviews is as important as the reviews themselves. It forces business leaders to ask questions, improve disciplines, and fix responsibility and accountability. It also forces them to reveal themselves. As the CFO, HR head, and I watched different leaders make their presentations at corporate reviews, we developed a clear sense of who was committed and knowledgeable, and who was not.

6. Live by the Vision of Leadership and Management

By embedding integrity processes inside business processes, the CEO and top business leaders show the company—in the most powerful, concrete terms—that "high performance with high integrity" is not simply a slogan, but is in fact the company's foundation. Personal involvement on the part of the CEO and the business leaders underscores the point: when they review risk-abatement plans for tough markets or new acquisitions, set integrity goals and objectives for key personnel, hold on-site integrity reviews, and communicate personally about major misses, they send a basic message: It really matters. "Do it . . . don't delegate it," says Ken Meyer, a former air force major general who today is one of GE's standout quality and integrity leaders. "Live it . . . don't preach it."

Principle 3: Adopt Global Ethical Standards

"Globalization through localization" is one of the mantras of transnational companies. "Localization," of course, includes adherence to the financial or legal rules of the specific national jurisdiction. GE's code of conduct begins: "Obey the applicable laws and regulations governing our business conduct worldwide."

But that's not always enough. In some cases, the answer to questions like "Is it according to GAPP?" or "Is it legal?" may not be adequate, because formal rules don't address the broad problems facing the company. Corporations may find the best answer is to go beyond required duties and voluntarily impose a higher global ethical standard on themselves and their employees. An organized, systematic process is needed to decide whether to adopt such global standards. Once adopted, these standards have the same uniform application and implementation across business units, product markets, and geographies as formal financial and legal rules. The following four practices speak to that challenge.

1. Understand Why You're Doing It

Corporations may adopt global standards beyond the requirements of formal rules for four broad, reenforcing reasons: reducing the risk of an integrity miss, improving the internal functioning of the company, creating advantages in markets, and enhancing the corporation's position in the broader global community.

Over the years, GE adopted a wide variety of global standards, typically for these reasons:

- Developing ethical sourcing policies that look not just at a supplier's technical and financial qualifications, but also at their systems, processes, and conditions relating to working conditions, child and prison labor, and environmental compliance. This produces better-quality, lower-risk suppliers, addresses objections to outsourcing like worker exploitation or environmental degradation, and enhances a corporation's general reputation.

- Applying nondiscrimination strictures relating to race, nationality, religion, and gender across the globe, which in many cases proves to be an important tool for recruiting and retaining high-potential employees.

- Prohibiting bribes and other forms of improper payments for all employees of both GE and company-controlled affiliates in a variety of public- and private-sector settings (consultants, gifts, political contributions), thereby making an unequivocal statement about honesty and fair dealing to employees.

- Building "greenfield" facilities outside the United States to industry or world environmental standards, thereby providing for better worker health and safety, protecting the plant location in particular and the environment in general, and reducing the risk of costly environmental cleanups.

- Establishing "responsible lending" standards in commercial finance that cover the business "wing-to-wing"—that is, from product development through advertising/sales/disclosure to applications/account servicing and collections/recovery—and thereby getting ahead of inexorable regulatory change, reducing risk, and enhancing the company's reputation.

- Minimizing the production of greenhouse gases and increasing internal energy efficiency, which not only protects the environment, but also provides an internal "proof statement" that GE's ecomagination technologies can actually help.

2. Identify the Issues

One way to identify possible global standards is to assess which issues are of vital importance for key stakeholders. Among other virtues, this keeps the question of global standards grounded in company realities. For example, tougher governance standards or greater financial transparency may be a persistent request of shareholders. Rebalancing short- and long-term debt, or imposing certain financial disciplines to maintain a Triple A rating, will be of significance to creditors. Introducing new requirements and processes in manufacturing facilities can improve employee health and safety. Special efforts to include women, minority, and non-U.S. candidates on slates for higher-level positions may positively affect an increasingly diverse employee and customer base. Developing products that reduce pollution beyond legal requirements is important to infrastructure customers, consumer end users, and broader communities. Yes, there may be conflicts within stakeholder groups (short-term versus long-term shareholders) or between stakeholders (shareholders versus creditors), but it's almost always better to get those issues on the table, at least for discussion purposes and possibly for resolution.

A second method for identifying possible global standards is to review the major global ethical codes, guidelines, and principles that have been promulgated by multilateral organizations, NGOs, or business groups, and determine which can have important benefits, if applied now to stakeholders. Again, this keeps the question grounded in the realities of the company, but it also avoids parochialism by drawing on the ideas of outsiders who have considered the issue. Sources include such compilations as the OECD Guidelines for Multinational Enterprises, the Caux Round Table Principles for Business, and the codes and policy guidelines of other global companies.[13]

An extremely helpful analysis for business leaders is the Global Business Standards Codex, developed by Harvard Business School professors Lynn Paine, Rohit Deshpande, and Joshua Margolis. It reviews both general and business-specific sources of global standards, and catalogues them under eight general principles (fiduciary, property, reliability, transparency, dignity, fairness, citizenship, and responsiveness). For those wishing to learn from what others have done, the codex is an excellent place to start.[14]

3. Assess Risk/Reward in a Societal Context

Deciding when to adopt global standards is not an abstract exercise, and it doesn't require the services of a senior vice president for political and moral philosophy. Such decisions should turn, instead, on a basic cost-benefit analysis rooted in the corporation's operations and culture. Note, however, that this involves a broader calculation than may normally be the case in corporate decision making. Note also that the decision will often require the discipline of a public explanation, including an analysis of the consequences if the company does, or does not, voluntarily adopt an ethical standard.

The concept of the *benefit* from global standards—in the company, in the marketplace, or in the broader society—can have many different meanings for the various stakeholders. It can involve everything from increasing operational excellence (by reducing pollution, customer complaints, employee lawsuits) to enhancing reputation (an intangible company asset), to fairness (treating all employees with dignity and respect), to avoiding harmful consequences to society (imminent injury from plant operations), to benefiting society in ways that also benefit business (philanthropic efforts to improve science and engineering education, or reducing greenhouse gases by developing new, profitable technologies).

Similarly, the concept of the *cost* of a global standard depends on context and should be analyzed as an investment. In some cases, there is clear financial cost—as in GE's efforts to reduce its own greenhouse gases and increase its efficiency in operations. But there may be enough savings from reduced energy use and payback from the demonstration of new and viable systems (e.g., the company's eco-magination technologies) to justify the investment in clear, quantifiable terms.

In other instances, the cost is extremely is hard to assess. How do you put a price on lost business resulting from a commitment to refrain from bribing? At the end of the day, GE viewed this hard-to-quantify cost as being far outweighed by common sense and hard-to-quantify benefits, including avoiding external enforcement risk and establishing an internal culture of integrity.

Thus, when a company is determining the costs and benefits of global ethical standards beyond the requirements of formal rules, a longer time frame than "quarterly results" or "this year's budget" may well be appropriate. The ultimate calculus may not be quantifiable, but may depend instead on commonsense judgment.

The GE global standards described above all were subject to this broader cost-benefit analysis. Take GE's ethical sourcing program. The company first qualified suppliers in terms of quality and financial health. It then added criteria relating to wages and working conditions, environmental programs, prison and child labor, and investing in methods and training. These techniques were then replicated as emerging market supply chains expanded. GE viewed these

costs over time to be easily outweighed by the benefits of reducing the risk of supply-chain interruption,
countering the globalization critics who looked for
evidence of labor exploitation, and enhancing the
company's general reputation as a responsible international player. An energetic debate took place within
the company as to whether and how to conduct such
sourcing. Ultimately, the hard numbers proved not
to be the controlling factor in the analysis.

4. Make Key Decisions at the Highest Level

In the end, decisions about global standards can't be
derived logically from some theory of moral philosophy, nor do they necessarily lend themselves to a
precise quantification. Judgment is essential. At GE,
Jeff Immelt formed a corporate risk committee of
top officers, which met quarterly, and which had decisions about global standards as one of its core responsibilities. In consultation with other top leaders,
the CFO and I set the agenda, seeking to put balanced analyses and realistic options in front of senior
management. Any of the committee's decisions that
were approved by the CEO and had significant operational or reputational implications—such as ethical
sourcing—were vetted by the board.

Elevating these decisions to the highest levels is
important. Why? Precisely because they don't turn

on discounted rates of return or abstract moral reasoning, but rather on commonsense judgments about avoiding risk or creating benefits in light of the company's history, culture, and mission.

Principle 4:
Use Early-Warning Systems to Stay Ahead of Global Trends and Expectations

Global travel and an unquenchable curiosity can help a CEO—and other senior leaders—maintain a "fingertip" sense of where the world is going. But to avoid surprises, corporations also need to gather information systematically on financial, legal, and ethical trends and expectations. (At GE, the impetus for this process came in the early '90s, following a series of highly publicized enforcement actions against other financial-services firms.) These "early-warning systems" can be put in place at all levels of the company—from P&L centers to large business units to the CEO's corporate risk committee—and the signals they send can be invaluable. Here are three core practices to help generate those signals.

1. Monitor Fast-Moving Financial and Legal Rules

The early-warning process for anticipating changes in formal financial or legal rules should have at least three phased aspects. First, experts in different areas of regulation affecting the business should continually mine sources around the world to monitor developments. These include new and pending legislation and regulation, filed and newly decided lawsuits, formal and informal governmental investigations, industry debates, consumer and other interest-group criticisms, and media reports on all of the above. A best practice is to hire a former regulator to "scrub the business" both for gaps under existing law and for potential issues, given the likely trajectory of public policy.

A second phase involves prioritizing these emerging issues and changing expectations, and presenting them to business-unit or division leaders for response. In consumer financial services, to cite just one example, changes are arising in different countries at different rates of speed with respect to a wide variety of issues, including interest rate ceilings, lending caps, and insurance product design and selling. Given that background, should there be more in-depth analysis? If so, what are the risks and costs of altering or not altering policies and practices?

The third phase, which of course is not always initiated, involves providing adequate resources to implement new policies and practices, and—every bit as important!—track the results.

Implementing this kind of early-warning system across a complex business unit—not to mention a huge, multibusiness, transnational corporation like GE—is a fundamental business process. It requires both input from specialists and constant attention from business leaders. Done right, however, it has significant value.

For example, by embracing this process, GE's huge financial-services arm has focused on an emerging financial-services "aiding and abetting" theory growing out of the Enron, WorldCom, and Parmalat fiascoes. Regulators have charged financial-services entities ("secondary actors") like JPMorgan, Citigroup, and Merrill Lynch with providing "substantial assistance" to customers (the "primary wrongdoer") whom the secondary actors allegedly knew (or should have known) were engaged in illegal or wrongful conduct (such as tax or accounting fraud). But the law remains unsettled with respect both to government enforcement and private suits.[15] "Substantial assistance" doesn't seem to be limited to actual participation in the illegal behavior. It can extend to knowledge of misdeeds by the primary wrongdoer, or even just ignoring red flags.

What *is* clear is that the consequences of "aiding and abetting" may be severe: criminal penalties for companies or individuals; enforcement remedies like injunctions, fines, disgorgement, or debarment; or large civil damage awards.

To avoid risk in this uncertain area, GE created significant systems for both its financial and its industrial businesses. Simply put, this effort defined the kinds of red flags to watch for (e.g. channel stuffing, side letters, and customer requests for incomplete certification), and laid out ways for employees to stay well clear of ambiguous areas by generating proper documentation and by escalating troublesome issues to experts.

2. Assess Emerging Demands for Ethical Corporate Action

A similar early-warning process applies to demands that the corporation take "ethical" actions extending beyond formal financial and legal requirements. These demands are emerging at an increasing rate from the stakeholder, NGO, and academic communities.

Again, it is important to sort these emerging ethical issues according to the type of stakeholder affected: from employees to shareholders and from customers to suppliers. For example, GE sought to pay close systemic attention to customer complaint patterns and to use "voice of the customer" sensing techniques.

Proposed new business strategies, products, or geographies may well have ethical dimensions, which should be expressly raised in the decision process.

For example: What are the implications of expanding in subprime lending at the same time the company is developing a responsible lending initiative? What are the implications of financing polluting plants at the same time that the company is trying to reduce its own greenhouse gases and increase energy efficiency?

Increasingly, corporations have a vice president for corporate citizenship, who— in consultation with functional experts and affected business leaders— serves as the focal point for aggregating and ranking these issues. High-priority questions should be analyzed thoroughly and then sent up to the CEO's corporate risk council for decisions about whether to accept voluntarily a new obligation not required by financial or legal rules. When GE revised its board-management governance principles in 2002, for example, it committed to an annual review of governance developments. Each October, possible changes are vetted with the board. If the stakeholder community makes a strong point about a governance issue—like majority rather than plurality voting for directors— change is likely to ensue.

Another important process for highlighting emerging ethical issues is the so-called common-sense review of the company's own practices. This technique was instituted at GE in 2005 as a result of the difficulties experienced by insurance broker Marsh & McLennan, when it failed to disclose adequately that it was receiving contingent commissions on both sides of some insurer/insured transactions—a problem affecting other brokers, as well. Some argued that MarshMac's incomplete disclosure of a potential conflict of interest to the affected parties was technically "lawful." But by the cold light of day, it was clearly a bad business practice.

GE now challenges its businesses to put the spotlight on ingrained business practices that raise questions in light of (1) evolving standards in the industry and (2) simple common sense. It asks whether these practices have both the appearance and the reality of being reasonable and ethical. For example: should credit-card interest rates be "disclosed" in credit babble and in small type, or should they be expressed in plain and legible English? GE's Aircraft Engines business used a "commonsense" review to identify a number of issues that required a response, including whether specific employment practices were invading employee privacy, whether certain "entertainment" expenses were excessive, and whether customers were improperly sharing GE technical information with competitors. When a practice flunked the commonsense test, it was modified or abandoned.

3. Address Evolving Reputational and Ethical Risks in Developing Nations

As a rule, transnational companies do business in any country if international law permits and if the commercial risk is acceptable. But of course, a company may choose not to do business in a nation that poses significant reputational and integrity risk. This was the case for the many U.S. businesses that withdrew from South Africa in the 1980s. But this is a tougher call in the early twenty-first century. Today, nations can sponsor terrorism, develop weapons of mass destruction (WMDs), engage in intracountry genocide, launder money, abuse human rights, deal in drugs, and otherwise make themselves pariahs on the international stage. So the basic issue—can we do business in this nation?—is very important and warrants another kind of early-warning process.

Such a process can start with the annual U.S. government lists of nations implicated in state-sponsored terrorism, WMDs, money laundering, drugs, and pervasive denial of human rights. These lists are matched against the company's present and planned commercial activity, and "watch-list nations" are identified. Expert sources are developed to predict likely political, economic, social, legal, and foreign policy developments in these high-risk nations. The company's senior staff person responsible for international policy runs the process, in consultation with senior staff and business leaders, and brings appropriate issues to the CEO.

For example: because Iran showed up on State Department lists of states sponsoring terrorism and seeking weapons of mass destruction, that nation earned a spot on GE's watch list. After continuous review, Jeff Immelt decided in 2004, with board approval, that GE would take no new orders in that country.

This may sound like an easy call, but it wasn't. GE's primary business in Iran, conducted through a wholly owned foreign subsidiary, was supplying pipeline equipment—mainly compressors—to major oil companies working in the Iranian fields. Sales were in the range of $300 million a year. Although direct U.S. sales already were barred under the Iran-Libya Sanctions Act, sales through such controlled foreign subsidiaries were allowed if there was no involvement by U.S. citizens, and if the U.S. content in the product was minimal. But Iran's support of the Iraq insurgency and serious questions about its potential development of atomic weapons made it difficult to defend sales simply because they were narrowly legal.

At the same time, important global oil-field customers were relying on supply from the GE subsidiary in Europe. Couldn't they fairly ask questions about GE's reliability as a partner, if the company unilaterally cut all ties to Iran? And if political scientists and academic ethicists find it difficult to make moral distinctions among nations (no to Iran, yes to Syria; yes to China, no to Myanmar), why should a transnational company find that task easy?

It's not easy. At the end of the day, GE chose to stop taking orders in Iran for a combination of business and nonbusiness reasons: the hostility of U.S. policy toward Iran; the increasing hostility of important institutional investors to corporations doing business in Iran; and, not least, the constant threat that Congress would eliminate the sales exception for foreign subsidiaries, which, if carried out, could make it impossible for GE to honor contracts and supply its customers.

Principle 5: Encourage the CFO and General Counsel to Be Both Partner and Guardian

At both the corporate and the business-unit levels, the financial and legal functions provide core checks and balances. They also play a key role in developing many of the processes needed for preventing, detecting, investigating, and remedying integrity violations—and for addressing broader business-in-society issues like governance, citizenship, public policy, and reputation. At the same time, of course, these functions—and especially the CFO and the GC—are deeply involved in helping to develop and execute key commercial strategies.

In other words, they must reconcile the sometimes contradictory roles of partner to the CEO and guardian of the corporation's integrity and reputation. Trying to strike this balance, and play both roles effectively, was certainly one of my biggest challenges at GE. But recognizing and dealing with that tension is absolutely essential, in the pursuit of high performance with high integrity. The CEO, in particular, has to encourage the CFO and the GC—as well as the HR leader, indeed all senior leaders—to play both roles energetically, especially at times of uncertainty and stress.[16]

In recent years, many CFOs and GCs have failed as guardians. In the financial scandals that began with Enron and centered on fraudulent accounting practices, a number of CFOs pled guilty to charges, were found guilty by juries, or resigned in disgrace. And although GCs didn't face charges as frequently, an insistent question was nonetheless raised: where were the lawyers? The answer is that either inside lawyers were excluded from key decisions or they failed to question aggressively whether problematic actions were legal or appropriate. In the options back-dating scandals, by contrast, both CFOs and GCs are in the dock.[17]

Many commentators have asked whether the in-side financial and legal functions—and by extension, the CFO and the GC—can ever serve effectively as guardians. The personal financial temptations—through cash compensation, options, restricted stock units, and other deferred compensation vehicles—can lead directly to corrupt acts. Or, less visibly, they can simply undercut the individual's ability to judge what is right for the corporation. At the same time, pressures exerted by the CEO and other senior leaders, and fear of reprisals ranging from firing to demotion to humiliation—at a time in one's career when family or other personal obligations may be at their highest—can affect one's independence and judgment.[18]

Can the CFO and the GC avoid being either a com-promised "yes" person or an excluded "naysayer"? I be-lieve deeply that it *is* possible to resolve the tension between being a partner and being a guardian, and that resolution is critical to carrying out each role. The key lies in building trust between the CEO and the key staff leader—easy to say, hard to do. Trust can't be de-manded; it has to be earned. But it has to grow out of conditions that the CEO must explicitly specify, and *mean*, which the CFO and the GC must meet, and which the board of directors must understand and approve.

Some examples follow.

1. Be a Strong Partner

For the CFO, the business role is central, as basic financial functions—financial analysis of operations and strategic choices, evaluation of deals, controllership, financial risk assessment, investor relations, and preparation of public financial statements—bring together the CEO and the CFO on a daily basis.

For the GC, the partnership role arises as he or she helps the CEO understand that the law can be used affirmatively and strategically in a wide variety of ways, including achieving business goals as quickly and effectively as possible, doing informative and constructive due diligence, helping to negotiate transactions, simplifying contracts while retaining needed protections, and helping to influence significant public policy debates. And as the GC learns the business, he or she may also participate effectively as a business person, rather than "just" a lawyer, in helping define and discuss key business issues.

2. Be a Strong Guardian

But, the CEO must also want both the CFO and the GC to be strong voices in raising issues relating both to performance risks and to integrity risks. With respect to the integrity risks, the CEO must recognize that both the CFO and the GC represent the corporation's interests—not the CEO's interests. In fact, to serve effectively as guardians, both the CFO and the GC should have strong independent relationships with the board. (By law, the general counsel represents the corporation, rather than the CEO.)[19]

In their guardian role, the CFO and the GC have to resist giving the kinds of quick, simplistic answers that may seem necessary in fast-moving, complex situations—deals, major negotiations, demands from government regulators, operational problems in emerging markets, product safety questions. The fundamental job is to help the CEO decide by finding key facts and conducting potent analysis. Of course, when presented with a black-and-white issue, they can and should answer quickly and forcefully: No, we can't improperly recognize revenue. No, we can't divide up markets with a competitor. By the same token, they must also have the experience and wisdom to give the go-ahead—without generating a memorandum to protect their rear—when they strongly support a proposed move.

But most mixed business-integrity issues come cloaked in shades of gray. The task of the CFO and the GC in such cases is to give the CEO options that—while all are lawful, and are all based on clearly articulated assumptions about the facts—entail varying degrees of legal, regulatory, ethical, and reputational risk. If more facts are needed, this has to be weighed against real-time pressures.

As GE's general counsel, I felt it was important to make and defend a recommendation—but only after articulating a range of "gray area" alternatives to the CEO, who would make the decision about how much integrity risk to take. This approach avoided the simplistic "no" answer and required me to work with others to develop business-integrity alternatives for achieving the performance goal. For example, if large health issues, such as asbestos contamination, were discovered in the course of a proposed acquisition, the temptation was to "just say no" to that deal. But we always looked for alternatives. For example, could we structure the transaction so the seller retained much, if not all, of the risk? This might not totally eliminate the problem for GE, but it would reduce it significantly. Even so, the CEO could ask, was the deal worth it?

3. Build Strong Finance, Legal, and HR Organizations

The partner-guardian roles—and the partner-guardian tension—flow down through the corporation. Like their counterparts at corporate, finance managers and division counsels must earn the trust of their business leaders to function both as partners and as guardians. The strength of the corporation depends on having world-class players—people with knowledge, experience, breadth, courage, and independence—deep in the organization.

This means that the CEO must support hiring the best possible people for these positions, even if they come from outside the company. At GE, Jack Welch (and then Jeff Immelt) supported my efforts to hire outstanding partners from private law firms who were experts in specialty areas (like tax, transactions, antitrust, or intellectual property) or who were broad M&A or litigation partners. Their formula was simple: pay market rates in cash comp and also offer a healthy slug of equity. They were convinced that the partner-guardian benefits of hiring the best down inside the company dramatically outweighed the costs—and their vision transformed inside law departments.[20]

A second key precept is that the "field" or "operational" lawyers are hired jointly by the business leader and the corporate CFO or GC but can be fired by either party—the "both hire, either fire" concept. In some companies, the legal and finance staffs are unitary and serve all business units. In others, they are decentralized, with business division leaders hiring their own staff. In either situation, both the business leader and the corporate CFO/GC need to agree on who serves the business leader—but the CFO/GC need to have an independent reporting relationship (straight line or strong dotted line) to ensure that line finance and legal people are properly discharging their partner-guardian roles.

4. Acknowledge Stress Points

Reconciling the tension between the partner-guardian roles involves the candid recognition of key stress points. Business leaders are by nature in a hurry—and, when under the hot whips of multiple pressures, may not have the patience for deep analysis or nuanced recommendations. Some of the toughest business-integrity issues come during crisis management, rather than in the stately process of strategic decision making. Group pressures may silence or dismiss a person trying to raise questions in a difficult situation, especially if that person's views are not fully formed and crisply stated. And of course, down the line, when business leaders begin to feel the pressure from above to meet performance goals, they may be less willing to consider integrity issues raised by peers or subordinates.

Then there's the role of the CEO. Almost invariably, CEOs test propositions by being skeptical, pushing back strenuously, asking hard questions, arguing the other side, and generally forcing people to defend their positions—as well they should! The stakes are high, and decision making at the highest levels has to be rough-and-tumble. All the more reason why the CFO and the GC must play the guardian role strenuously, unafraid to answer candidly or argue back, undaunted by personal or group pressure, and secure within their thick skins. They can't let their views be summarily dismissed in the heat of battle. They have to get those views on the table, understood, and considered in the decision process.

5. Emphasize the Importance of the Dual Role

CEOs must leave no doubt on any corporate level that they really want candid, unvarnished, forceful presentations of options relating to financial, legal, ethical, and reputational risk. They can accomplish this in a number of ways:

- By hiring independent, credible people to serve as CFO and GC—people with strong reputations for effectiveness and integrity, and with the demonstrated ability to build strong organizations.

- By making it clear to the company in all meetings—from the smallest of decision groups to the grandest of corporate set pieces—that they expect leaders (and especially the staff leaders) to serve both as partners in the business enterprise and as guardians of the corporation.

- By making it clear to the CFO and the GC in particular, from the initial hiring conversations to performance and compensation reviews, that they want and expect thoughtful and candid guardians who are also expert and effective partners.

- By making the CEO's commitment to the dual role clear to the board: agreeing on CFO/GC job descriptions, having select directors meet final CFO or GC candidates, and scheduling regular sessions for the CFO and the GC to meet with the board alone, thereby underscoring for the board's benefit the independent aspect of the dual role.

The complex elements of chemistry and trust that must exist between the CEO and staff leaders are hard to describe and harder yet to mandate. But it is one of the most important dimensions of a high-performance, high-integrity company. My personal goal with both Jack Welch and Jeff Immelt was not to be their pal. It was to have a strong, respectful personal and professional relationship in which they wanted me to speak my mind on what was best for the company. I was very fortunate. Even when meetings were hot or stress was high, and despite their very different personal styles, they both wanted it straight.

Principle 6: Foster Employee Awareness, Knowledge, and Commitment

A high-performance-with-high-integrity culture rests on the commitment of all employees

- To understand their formal and ethical obligations

- To do things right by following those duties

- To do the right thing by living the values of candor, honesty, fairness, reliability, and trustworthiness

The most fundamental learning comes from simply observing how their peers and leaders handle tough, stressful situations with integrity. But for many subjects, the company needs to help employees become aware of the risks, show them how to find the right answer, and reinforce their commitment to do the right thing.

Educating employees about these issues is an extremely challenging proposition—one that is often given lip service, but less often given creative thought. This is truly a lost opportunity. In a typical year, GE (to cite just one example) hires more than twenty thousand professionals, takes on thousands more through acquisitions, and promotes still others to new cross-border jobs. Many of these people joined the company to get education and training that could help advance their careers—for example, in engineering, finance, marketing, sales, and technology development. CEOs proudly extol their company's "learning" culture.

But the typical "integrity training" program has less appeal. Especially to multicultural employees with little background in "business in society" issues, these programs can seem irrelevant, sterile, and boring. The CEO and the company's leaders must give equal pride of place to integrity skills and business skills—and, indeed, must look for ways to teach these two kinds of skills together, whenever possible, in a true "learning company." Such training must candidly confront the long-standing rationalizations that employees use for improper conduct, especially in emerging markets: it's the custom here; it is not really illegal; no one will know; the company condones it; there won't be consequences.[21]

1. Articulate the Word

The first, crucial step in education and training is to articulate "the word": *what people should do*. Simple as this is to say, it involves a complex flow-down of precepts on financial, legal, and ethical issues. It may entail, for example:

- A simple, clear code of conduct that articulates the basic aspirations of the company. GE's one-page code tried to express the essentials under the rubric *everywhere, every day, everyone*: "Obey the applicable laws and regulations governing our business conduct worldwide . . . Be honest, fair, and trustworthy in all your activities and relationships . . . Through leadership at all levels, sustain a culture where ethical conduct is recognized, valued, and exemplified by all employees." But this is just the first step in a journey of a thousand miles.

- A complementary policy guide that sets forth basic integrity policies applying to all employees, all around the globe, on tough subjects like unfair competition, bribery, conflicts of interest, environmental damage, unethical sourcing, invasions of privacy, and money laundering. Such a guide should describe not only what to do, but what to watch out for (red flags). It should describe salient real-world problems and provide answers. At GE, we called our guide the *Spirit and Letter*, with the "spirit" setting out broad themes and core values like honesty, candor, fairness, reliability, and trustworthiness, and the "letter" describing global integrity policies in detail on the Web. The guide was translated into thirty-one languages.

• For critical cross-company issues, much more detailed implementing guidelines to address thorny, recurring issues—like improper payments, supplier relationships, distributor relationships, or fair competition. At GE, writing these detailed guides forced us think through uniform company positions on the kinds of difficult problems that employees and leaders on the front lines raised frequently— things like demands for political contributions and requests from a member of a country's ruling family to be taken on as a partner. Additionally, GE developed a host of detailed business-specific policies and guidelines—for NBC, Energy, Aircraft Engines, Consumer

Finance, and so on—which required the same kind of thought and effort.

The "word" is not just about what to do, but also why to do it. And this "why" has two dimensions: why the rule exists, and why it is important to the company. I believe that without these "whys," the "what" lacks punch. The reason? Because it fails to treat people with respect. People don't just want commands; they need explanations and understanding.

2. Deliver It

The fundamental question described above remains, How does a company deliver the essence of these integrity precepts so that people know *and* feel the message? Multiple and mutually reinforcing steps are needed.

- Candid orientation underscores that these issues are not just Dilbertian rhetoric, but real. At GE, we began the session for every new hire and newly acquired employee with an eighteen-minute video produced by NBC and narrated by a major on-air talent. But it was far from "rah-rah," self-righteous stuff. Instead, in vivid, dramatic terms, the film described serious mistakes people in the company had made—for example, the Israel procurement fraud and the Japan data tampering—and the serious consequences that followed. The goal was to grab people emotionally and depict honestly the types of problems that arise in a complex global company.

- A tracking, training, and testing system (which I called "3T") is essential. Every position is risk-assessed for the type of training materials required. This can range from the basic level 1 *Spirit and Letter* materials that went to everyone, to much more sophisticated level 2 training for people in "at risk" positions: from plant managers with complex environmental responsibilities to salespeople in tough environments like Russia or China. Each employee is tracked when he or she moves to a new position. Within a fixed number of days, they must take online training. The training includes a testing component to see whether the information was absorbed. Employees are tracked, retrained, and retested periodically, especially if they are in high-risk positions, because without retention of awareness, knowledge, and commitment, the whole exercise is pointless.

- Case-based learning grabs both minds and hearts. Putting people into tough case situations—your competitor accidentally leaves a copy of his bid book in the customer's conference room—forces them to grapple with competing forces and considerations, to try on different roles, and to look for alternative ways to approach the problem. This kind of learning can be delivered as an interactive Web program, but there is no substitute for resource-intensive, face-to-face training by experienced teachers, preferably from within the company.

- Using actual failures or successes has enormous impact. We found there was an exponentially greater impact when business leaders presented actual cases of inappropriate action—either in person at senior staff meetings or throughout the organization via Web messaging. We tried to put prurient interest to work in a good cause. Changing the facts just enough to disguise identities, these presentations laid bare the root causes of the problem, explained the disciplinary actions that ensued, and described remedies that grew out of the case.

- In my experience, the integration of integrity skills training with business skills training is optimal. When teaching employees about submitting government bids or making foreign procurements, for example, the integrity dimension should be "baked in" to grab employee attention and to demonstrate the importance of fusing high performance with high integrity. At GE, the energy business developed a best-practice Web site, Sales Channels University, which combined business and ethics training.[22]

3. Address Cultural Differences Head-On

Integrity education and training across the globe must identify and candidly address local cultural practices that are (or appear to be) at sharp variance with the corporation's global norms. For example, due to the tragic consequences in Europe of collaboration with ruthless, totalitarian secret police—for example, the Gestapo under the Nazis and the postwar Stasi in East Germany—European employees of a certain age are reluctant to use the ombuds system to report concerns about fellow employees to the company. Frankly acknowledging that history and explaining how the ombuds system is different—information will be handled fairly and may not be used for political vendettas—begins to address a deep-seated issue. But there is no substitute for hiring highly respected local employees to perform the ombuds role, which they then explain to their fellow workers. (I'll describe the ombuds system at greater length below.)

Similarly, in Asia, awarding business to family members or "greasing" a deal may be a local cultural norm. Newly hired employees may have worked in local, or even global, corporations that tolerate these practices. Companies have to design programs that don't heap scorn on local culture (and, by implication, on our employees, their families, and their friends), but rather explain why those practices are unacceptable in a global company. Training for third parties in different cultures—suppliers, joint venture partners, distributors, consultants—is also necessary (but difficult).[23]

4. Design Special Leadership Education and Training

A separate leaders' guide to integrity—a special "word" for leaders—should set forth basic leadership responsibilities both for general principles and practices (prevention, detection, response) and for specific policy areas (e.g., fair employment, export controls). Every senior executive in the corporation should also have specially tailored leadership training appropriate to their business, their job, their competitors, and their geography within a defined period after assuming their position. Retraining may be required if an individual moves to a job in a different business or market, with a required refresher course—even without moves—scheduled for every two or three years.

In the contentious world of the global economy, companies should also design broader, special courses for young, emerging leaders on business and society issues: debates about citizenship, the ways government impacts competition and profitability, public policy processes in different nations, ways to think about business ethics, and country political risk. Most leaders have come up through specialist ranks without a broader view, and most companies (GE included) don't provide such training in any depth—or at all.

At GE, the target population for leadership training is the top 4,000 people (200 officers, 400 senior executives, and 3,300 executives). Initial leadership training lasts at least a one full day. A desktop-based leadership self-assessment tool, developed by GE businesses, is aimed at stimulating action. It asks leaders a series of detailed questions about their actions along six dimensions: personal engagement, risk assessment and mitigation, concern reporting and resolution, evaluations—*and* comprehensive education and training coupled with a broader high-performance-with-high-integrity communications strategy.[24]

Principle 7: Give Employees Voice

One of the most powerful principles in creating a high-performance-with-high-integrity culture, and for ensuring accountability up and down the corporation, is to give every employee "voice." This means encouraging (and, indeed, requiring) the reporting of concerns about possible violations of financial, legal, and ethical standards, and addressing those concerns promptly.

Contrast this with the "culture of silence" described by Boeing's GC in a blistering January 2006 speech—given to top management at the request of newly arrived CEO Jim McNerney—as a significant cause of the company's document-theft and conflict-of-interest scandals.[25] Indeed, in most of the scandals in recent years, employees knew about troublesome behaviors, but either were afraid to give voice to their concerns or were unable to do so because no one would listen. Whether we look at Enron's off-balance-sheet entities, or WorldCom's fraud, the problem could have been addressed far sooner and the damage could have been far less if the corporation had the capacity to receive and treat employee concerns seriously.

The employees' voice can be expressed through at least four channels.

1. The Ombuds System

Virtually every oral and written integrity communication to employees, starting with the fundamental integrity guide, should stress the importance of reporting concerns, and spotlight the "ombuds system." At GE, the ombudsperson is a neutral intake person chosen on the basis of personal skills, rather than functional expertise, because trust is critical. The ombudsperson:

- Refers matters raising integrity concerns to financial, legal, and HR staffs for investigation

- Tracks all such matters to ensure prompt close-out

- Keeps the employee up-to-date on the status of the concern

The word *concern* is more appropriate than *possible violation* or *charge* because it encourages people to report broadly on ethical and reputational questions as well as formal policy issues—and it is better to have more, rather than fewer, reports.

The corporate ombudsperson oversees other corporate ombudspersons around the world (Europe, Asia, Middle East, Latin America) as well as a system of ombudspersons in each of the global businesses.

GE has more than six hundred persons in some forty-five nations doing this job—some full-time, some part-time—and the system can receive concerns in thirty-one languages. In recent years, approximately fifteen hundred concerns have been reported annually, with about 50 percent simply seeking information, but about 20 percent leading to serious disciplinary action.

An effective system has these elements:

- **Employees should be strongly encouraged to report concerns immediately, through corporate or business ombudspersons or functional staff, using integrity help lines, letters, phone, or e-mail.** Employees can report anonymously, if they so chose. All concerns are docketed centrally in the ombuds system.

- **Employees have a duty to report concerns— and not to retaliate.** The ombuds system only works if (1) employees have an obligation to report concerns, and (2) failure to do so leads to discipline, including termination in cases where very serious matters (e.g., improper payments, accounting fraud) are left unreported. The corollary—again explained in all integrity communications—is that retaliation is an equally serious offense, with termination as the likely result.

- **Finance and legal staffs must fully, fairly, and promptly investigate all concerns without fear or favor.** Corporate politics or other internal pressures can't be allowed to interfere with finding the facts (in a prompt and professional manner) and making independent recommendations about individual discipline and system changes. If allegations relate to people at the top of the company, the CFO or the GC may recommend to the CEO or to the board that outside investigators be retained to avoid any potential conflicts of interest.

- **The ombuds system's important cases and statistical summaries should be regularly reported to the CEO and the board.** Issues arriving through the company help line and the director hotline mandated by Sarbanes-Oxley should be reported separately.[26]

2. Business "Bottom-up" Reviews

A second way to give employees voice is an annual "bottom-up" review: an important component of each business's broader, periodic integrity review. At

GE, this review starts with on-the-ground employees in each nation. Either finance, legal, or their managers ask them about risks they perceive or issues they might have with the integrity infrastructure. This review then builds up through localities, countries, and regions, giving employees higher in the organization the same opportunity to assess the business's integrity efforts. (Concerns about individual behavior are directed to the ombuds system.) It culminates in a report on results for the global division as a whole that identifies in rank order which risks, policies, and processes have registered the most questions or comments.[27]

3. An Elite Corporate Audit Staff

This staff is one of the most important assets of the corporation, and it can serve as another important channel for employees to raise concerns. The audit staff focuses on fundamental controllership issues: financial integrity (e.g., balance sheet, account reconciliation, controllership processes, and capacity), compliance with legal and ethical precepts, and risk management. It also focuses on salient issues in a growth setting: due diligence, acquisition integration, and dispositions. It spends about 80 percent of its time auditing for adherence to global financial, legal, and ethical standards, including issues in tough realms like third parties, remote sites, information technology, and government contracts. During the course of the year's work, the audit staff comes in contact with a wide variety of employees. It hears their concerns about their business's systems, processes, and practices, especially those that they may not wish to voice in the business's own bottom-up review, or which may be too complex for an ombuds report. The audit staff reports regularly to the CFO, the company compliance review board, and the audit committee—both on systemic issues and on important questions raised by employees.

GE's corporate audit staff (CAS) has a long, distinguished record. In 2007, it numbered more than five hundred, with about 50 percent non-U.S. citizens. It operated in forty-four countries, and covered 95 percent of all GE assets in a rolling two-year period. In addition, the CAS has always been viewed as an important gateway to company leadership. CAS alums step into key business jobs (often in finance), and almost 20 percent of GE's two hundred officers are graduates of the audit staff, where they learned the fundamentals of fusing high performance with high integrity.

4. The Strong Dotted Line in Finance and Legal

There is a long tradition in GE that the finance managers and general counsels in the business—and indeed, all finance and legal staff—have not only a direct line to the division business leader, but also a very strong dotted line to the company CFO and GC (and in the case of human resources, to the corporate HR leader). GE expects that division finance and legal staff will "report up the line" and consult with the CFO, the GC, or other senior corporate finance and legal leaders when significant questions about commercial, legal, ethical, and reputational risks arise within their units. The corporate functional leaders assess whether there is a problem, consult with their business counterparts about how to handle it, and—if it cannot be resolved promptly at the division level—discuss how to elevate it to the CEO.

Keeping these lines of communication open is not easy. Again, it depends on two-way trust. The CFO and the GC (and the HR leader) must earn the trust of their business-unit counterparts—and business-unit leaders—by first being true counselors: listening, asking questions, testing ideas, and suggesting possible actions. They have to resist the temptation to assert control over the matter by "running to the CEO." Of course, significant and time-sensitive matters must go to the CEO (or the board), but the CFO or the GC can help the business take the lead in doing that.

In return, the business-unit CFOs and GCs must honor their obligation to "report up" on serious concerns—even though there is a constant temptation to guard their relationship with the division business leader by hoarding information. Corporate has to stress that the business finance manager, lead lawyer, or HR leader has a positive obligation to alert the corporate CFO, GC, or HR leader about serious financial, legal, ethical, or reputational concerns. A reporting-up failure is cause for serious sanctions, including termination. The strong dotted line means that the company's CFO, GC, and HR leader can help ensure that this happens, because they have an important voice in their business counterparts' cash compensation, equity grants, and promotion.

These four channels are all part of a larger effort to create an open and candid company. At GE, they run in parallel with "work-outs," which encourage employees to critique and rebuild basic company processes. By giving genuine voice to individuals throughout the company, and by treating their concerns with respect and professionalism, business leaders from the CEO on down send a potent message about the importance of a self-cleansing culture: one that promptly surfaces what is wrong and candidly discusses what is right.

This "collective" voice of employees doesn't just detect; it also deters. An unethical business leader nearing the end of a tough quarter has to think twice before urging accounting impropriety on his team, and perhaps precipitating an integrity investigation.

My experience over many years was that these channels were rarely misused and did not create a climate of fear and backbiting. Reporting employees knew from long-standing company experience that their concerns would be handled independently, reviewed professionally, and decided fairly based on facts, not internal politics. Cheap shots wouldn't work.

Principle 8: Pay for Performance with Integrity

The challenge for companies is not just to reward financial performance. The ultimate goal must be a compensation system that pays for performance with integrity. Of course, most companies *claim* that they build integrity issues into their compensation and promotion decisions. But how many companies use meaningful evaluation tools so that real accountability for integrity takes root? And how many companies extend the use of these beyond the corporate officers to the top echelon of P&L leaders or to key players on business teams?

Four key practices can make this principle come alive.

1. Use Annual Goals and Objectives —and Evaluations

The place to start is building integrity issues into annual goals and objectives for senior leaders. For example: solving integrity problems identified in due diligence, hiring a needed Environmental Health and Safety (EHS) specialist, reducing the number of third-party distributors in a difficult market to lower the risk of improper payments, minimizing customer or employee complaints, or deftly handling a controversy. The CEO should discuss these specific annual integrity objectives with direct reports, identify them as a basis for compensation, and evaluate them systematically at year end—just as with performance goals.

2. Assess the Leader's Own Program

Corporations need to evaluate business leaders on their efforts to create fundamental high-performance-with-high-integrity systems, processes, and culture in their unit or division. The core principles and practices provide the necessary standards: the strength of the integrity infrastructure, the strength of employee voice, the adequacy of early-warning systems, or the hiring of "A" players, to name a few. GE used a variety of evaluation techniques: corporate audits, ombuds statistics, employee surveys, on-site reviews by corporate leaders both in the United States and in the rest of the world, corporate personnel reviews, formal reviews of businesses by the corporate compliance review board, the handling of difficult controversies or problems, and how the leader responded to a crisis. Many of these assessments—such as ombuds reports or plant EHS data—have a quantitative dimension, and year-over-year comparisons within the business itself can be an important yardstick. Finally, the self-assessment tool used in leadership training articulates a detailed series of actions against which leaders can be evaluated.[28]

3. Use Comparative Assessments

Another potent method of performance-with-integrity evaluation is to compare the leader's business with other businesses within the multibusiness corporation or—where information is available—with peer companies. These comparisons can be based on the audit staff reviews of the whole company (e.g., which business has the most open audit issues), the overall number of relevant lawsuits filed, or former regulators' assessments of a business against industry standards and best practices.

Cross-unit comparisons on financial and legal integrity issues are a powerful way to evaluate and motivate business leaders—especially when the company's top leaders, at their regular meetings, review charts comparing their performance. How do the leaders rank on the number of audit adjustments required in a year, and how quickly do they close open audit items? How do they compare on the number of actionable concerns registered in the ombuds system, or on the audit staff's review of integrity programs in Asia?

At GE, the corporate environmental group's digitized reporting system allowed the CEO to compare every plant and every business on a host of EHS parameters—with the bottom quartile receiving "coffins" around the relevant numbers (e.g., permits missed, unlawful discharges) and the top quartile receiving "halos."

Another key comparative tool for assessing leadership is the annual employee survey. In 2006, more than 127,000 professional employees across GE were asked in an anonymous survey (that generated a 95 percent response rate) whether they agreed or disagreed with the statement "There are no compromises around here when it comes to conducting business in an ethical way." For GE as a whole, 85 percent agreed, and 5 percent disagreed. But these numbers varied across business units, and those variances raised important questions about the intensity and effectiveness of leadership. For example, when 23 percent of responders in a GE regional survey said leaders were more concerned with results than compliance, change came swiftly: new leaders, a new compliance staff, a reorganized ombuds system, and more visits by the audit staff.

4. Make It a Clear Factor in Compensation and Promotion

Success in meeting annual goals, assessments of the overall program both on its own terms and comparatively, qualitative evaluations of intensity and commitment—the CEO can use these measures and more to develop standards to pay for performance with integrity, working with the board's compensation committee. For example, expected performance in this area could constitute 20 to 30 percent of both cash compensation (salary and bonus) and equity grants.

Poor performance would diminish either the rate of increase or the absolute year-over-year amounts— or lead to a firing, if a senior leader violated integrity policies or failed to create an integrity culture. Conversely, superior performance—creating new systems and processes or working through a difficult problem that threatens the company's reputation— can be among the plus factors leading to positive annual increases and promotions.

Of course, compensation and promotion decisions are always going to be matters of judgment. But personalized goals and objectives plus explicit integrity compensation guidelines—which affect a component of pay and are factors in promotions—provide the essential, real-world incentives that can have a significant role in creating the high-performance-with-high-performance culture. They can turn a corporate cliché—integrity is considered in compensation decisions—into a core corporate principle.

IV. The Toughest Issues

The core principles and practices described in the previous section apply across the broad range of business operations. But they are particularly significant in dealing with recurring, complex, and vexing issues of this global era—issues that demand special CEO attention. These include emerging markets, acquisitions, crisis management, public policy, and reputation.

I'll consider these issues separately in the following pages. It's worth noting, though, that they are interrelated. A good reputation grows out of effective crisis management and defensible positions on public policy. Integrity in emerging markets depends, in part, on the effective integration of acquisitions.

Emerging Markets

During my time at GE, whenever I was asked what I lost sleep over, my answer was always the same: emerging markets.

In a sense, multinationals have conjured up a dilemma. For understandable reasons, they have embraced the potential of significant new growth in the developing world, touting it at analysts' meetings and in public speeches. (GE Asia's revenues were projected to grow from $18 billion to $36 billion between 2004 and 2008.) At the same time, they are quietly aware of the significant integrity and country risk minefields that threaten to impair performance and destroy margins: limited rule of law, endemic corruption, rampant conflicts of interest, erratic enforcement, money laundering, unscrupulous local competitors, and hard-to-assess economic and political risk. To meet their dramatic growth projections, transnational companies must navigate treacherous shoals.

Four practices are essential.

1. Build (and Insist Upon!) a Uniform Global Culture

The temptation to bend the rules in tough markets is great, especially for employees from the local culture. But the fundamental position for a transnational company aspiring to high performance with high integrity is crystal clear: across all international markets, the company culture must demand strict adherence to formal financial and legal rules, whether local or international, to the company's global ethical standards and to the employee values of honesty, candor, fairness, trustworthiness and reliability.

Easy to say, hard to do; nevertheless, the uniform precept cannot be compromised. Why? Because in a global company, with leaders and employees moving from nation to nation, the hypocrisy of selectively ignoring particular rules or standards—or treating different countries differently—fatally corrodes the fundamental value of integrity for *all* employees.

Some multinationals choose not to enforce global policies but instead to "decentralize" values and integrity, and let local managers "adapt" to local conditions. It's a bad approach. This look-the-other-way decentralization, despite companywide rhetoric, was an important contributor to Siemens's towering bribery scandal (hundreds of millions of dollars in improper payments in various business units) that led to the departure of the board chair and the CEO, and has created turmoil across the company.[1]

Implementing the fundamental principles and practices discussed in section II across various businesses in the wide variety of emerging markets—with their different histories, cultures, institutions, and practices—takes time, effort, and money. This is especially true when the corporation begins to move from an export sales strategy to a strong local manufacturing, distribution, and sourcing strategy, as so many are doing. A laser focus on process mapping, risk assessment, risk mitigation, and controllership is essential. Top company leadership simply can't throw the emerging market dilemma in the laps of emerging market leaders, demand stretch performance targets, and hope for the best.

So granular, realistic estimates of the costs of building the integrity infrastructure must be baked into the numbers, after review by global business leaders who are responsible for creating an enduring emerging market organization. Without that consistent message from the top and without realistic business plans, the pressures for local leaders in emerging markets to seek performance and ignore integrity may simply be too great.

2. Spotlight the Endemic Problems

To achieve high performance with high integrity, the CEO and the business and functional leaders must spotlight special endemic risks. These include, for example, acquisitions, improper payments, sourcing, export control regimes, conflicts of interest, environmental health and safety, competitor contacts, and nepotism. To head off problems in these realms, GE developed explicit policies, guidelines, education and training, checklists, and checks and balances beyond the basic performance-with-integrity systems and processes. Of course, each issue in each country presents its own complexities, but three brief examples—focusing on improper payments, remote sites, and sourcing in the global supply chain—can help illustrate the general approach.

Improper Payments. These come in many guises: direct bribes, payments to unsavory agents for help with government contracts, unlawful political or charitable contributions, inappropriate gifts and entertainment, company-financed vacations masquerading as "business trips," and many more. Most multinational corporations have paper policies—whether based on U.S. or local law—prohibiting payments of this sort. But the challenge is to create a real program that reaches real employees and speaks to their real issues.

For example, the use of consultants or agents in government procurements—often required by local governments—is a fertile ground for abuse. In such cases, genuine due diligence is vital. Is the agent in-country? Does he have industry expertise? Are there obvious conflicts of interest? What is his reputation? How does the embassy view him? Is the fee within reasonable commercial limits? Is payment directed to a "clean" or a suspicious account? Can the work be specified? Are the contracts written to require consultants to certify ethical conduct, creating the company's right both to audit and to terminate, as necessary?

GE employees are trained to "have their eyes open," and are required to report requests for cash, inflated invoices, requests for customer-appointed partners or suppliers, and payments to third parties. Obviously, this is a difficult area. Recognizing that, the company recently has held summits for top employees in sensitive regions like the Middle East and Asia on third-party agents and distribution. The goal of these summits is to spread best practices, establish a consistent, cross-business approach on when to use third parties, implement automated monitoring, improve agent and distributor training, and develop goals and techniques for reducing use of such third parties by as much as 30 percent in the near term.[2]

Remote Sites. Remote sites, where controllership and supervision tend to be attenuated, are a recurrent source of performance-with-integrity issues. Problems include misappropriation of funds, lack of proper third-party employment contracts, favoritism or retaliation in these small offices, and poor accounting systems. This emerged as a high-priority issue for GE as it expanded in emerging markets (and as problems mounted). Assessment tools were developed to rank risk at sites. Special disciplines—from cash management to SWAT team controllership reviews to special emphasis on the compliance infrastructure for new employees—were applied to the highest-risk locales.

Sourcing in the Global Supply Chain. This issue has received close scrutiny at GE as it increased exponentially over the past decade. As the company was first ramping up global sourcing in the mid-90s, clothing and toy manufacturers got into serious controversies over their sourcing practices. Observing this development, we concluded that before too long, the issue would affect all global businesses. We felt we had a basic responsibility not to support "outsourced" practices that GE itself would not engage in—to protect workers, to guard our reputation, and to sustain support for global economic integration.

An extensive sourcing white paper and other materials provide guidance to those in the field on the key program elements and hard issues: the relevant standards (e.g., no workers below minimum age, compliance with EHS laws or standards); due diligence protocols both at qualification and requalification; clear assignment of responsibility to sourcing leaders to manage the process; proper responses when nonconformances occur; how to monitor during the contract; and standards for second- and third-tier suppliers. Supply-chain integrity failures (most recently in imported food, medicine, and toys from China) have serious brand, reputational, and financial consequences for many companies, indicating that integrity concerns surrounding sourcing will be on the front burner for the foreseeable future.

3. Insist on Good Education and Training —and Good People

As mentioned earlier, GE felt it had to address cultural issues head-on. For example, we had to convince Europeans to overcome their historical distaste for reporting to authorities and use the ombuds system. Equally, we had to convince Asians that family partners had to be disclosed and approved. We struggled to counter employee attitudes in emerging markets that practices are more important than law, or that they will not be caught, or that if caught, it doesn't matter.

But these particular issues point to the larger challenge: finding the people, message, method, and evaluations that collectively constitute a culturally sensitive yet globally effective set of communications in each market. Here, especially, face-to-face sessions with employees unschooled in the company's global culture are essential; Web or paper training is second best. For example, GE Healthcare developed a short training case about the now famous (but fictitious) Mr. Vu, who faced multiple tough scenarios: hiring third-party consultants, approving travel and living expenses, dealing with customers' demands for bribes, and the use of the GE mark.

Again, such learning by example isn't easy. Knowledgeable trainers, who themselves have the benefit of time and training, are necessary to develop trust and to provide the benefit of illuminating, energized discussions. GE has found it very hard to match the exponential growth in Asian employees with live, in-context training and has had to settle, too often, for a Web-based approach.

This challenge is mirrored in the difficulty of finding multilingual, multicultural leaders who can help the corporation act with both local sensitivity and global discipline in emerging markets while also anticipating contingencies, diversifying operations, and finding still more good people. These leaders are increasingly subject to "raids" by competitors, other MNCs, or globalizing local companies. The tightening labor market in developing nations for sophisticated local managers and professionals creates one of the biggest performance—and integrity—challenges for global companies.

4. Make the Hard Choices

Multinational corporations will always experience tensions between local practices and global standards. These tensions often lead to hard choices.

One such choice arises when local customer practices are at variance with local laws. For example, using ultrasound technology for abortions on the basis of the gender of the fetus is against the law in both China and India—but is nonetheless widely practiced, due to the importance placed in those cultures on male offspring. This is a hot-button issue in parts of those societies—and around the world. Medical equipment manufacturers like GE had to determine how to sell ultrasound equipment, which of course has many legitimate medical purposes, into a market characterized by its illegal use.

Steps included educating customers, putting warning labels on equipment, writing product manuals that highlighted legal requirements, selling only to physicians licensed and certified in compliance with the law, and providing sales data to appropriate state and central authorities who are just now beginning to enforce the law. GE could not guarantee that its ultrasound equipment was not being used illegally for sex-selection abortions, but it could point to serious, good-faith efforts to forestall that outcome.

A second kind of hard choice arises when local law—which multinationals are required to obey—comes into conflict with a company's global standards. After arresting a GE employee for demonstrating in Tiananmen Square against the Chinese government's prohibition against Falun Gong, local Chinese law enforcement authorities asked to search the computers of all employees at the demonstrator's GE unit to see whether they had ties to that group. GE declined, because the request conflicted with the company's global standards of respect for employee personal privacy and religious freedom, and because acquiescence would open GE to the international charge of complicity in a human rights violation. In this particular case, GE was able to avoid a direct conflict by persuading the local investigators (after some discussions in Beijing) to drop their request, arguing that the company had a worldwide policy against political solicitations or religious proselytizing in the workplace, and that the government could precipitate a political incident if it forced GE to allow the requested invasion of religious freedom and privacy—or forced GE to say no formally.

But such dilemmas may not be headed off when the impact extends beyond a single work unit. In one recent and notable case, Google—determined to compete with a Chinese search engine—chose to abide by

Chinese censorship law, which was in conflict with its broad ethical principles against such governmental restrictions. For example, users in China were directed to nonpolitical content when entering the word "Tiananmen," while users in the United States, whether using English or Chinese, were routed to sites that had content about controversial political events. The decision sparked a broad global debate. Was this an indefensible compromise of basic business principles or was it justified on the grounds that, if it chooses to do business in a foreign nation, a multinational company must follow the law of that country; that it was thus the only way for Google to compete in China; and that even a trammeled access to information on the Internet ultimately pushes China toward more freedom of expression?[3]

A third kind of hard choice arises when corrupt practices in a nation are so pervasive that conflicts with global rules or global standards cannot be resolved, and the corporation has to ask whether it must exit particular industries—or leave the country entirely. At various times, for example, GE has chosen not to do business in Iran (an alleged state sponsor of terrorism and supporter of insurgents in Iraq), in Colombia (where employees' safety cannot be guaranteed and money laundering is rife), and in "cash-flow businesses" in Russia (a locus of widespread organized crime and money laundering).

Acquisitions

Evaluating acquisitions carefully, and then integrating them effectively into a larger corporate portfolio, is essential for performance—and for performance with integrity.

The acquisition teams address a host of business problems: from reconciliation of the financials to detailed operational transfers to employment and pension issues. But they also must tackle integrity issues, ranging from culture to systems and processes to specific financial, legal, and ethical problems. Without effective due diligence and integration, acquisitions fail to meet pro forma projections—often badly—for both business and integrity reasons. In recent years, more than 50 percent of the GE corporate audit staff's investigations stemmed from problems associated with deals, especially in emerging markets.

Three fundamental practices help acquisitions meet expectations—and perform with integrity.

1. Create a Robust Process

In a typical year, GE spends more than $20 billion on acquisitions. Not surprisingly, it has devoted significant time and effort developing detailed processes to minimize cultural, operational, and integrity risks and to increase synergies and performance beyond the deal pro formas.

The GE approach is explicitly divided into distinct phases: evaluation, due diligence, negotiations and signing, further diligence plus integration planning, closing, acquisition integration, and transition to operations. At each of these stages, an interrelated set of very specific tasks is laid out in specific functions (commercial, operations, finance, HR, IT, etc.) under an overall deal team head, and then an integration leader. Tasks include summarizing the deal rationale, articulating success criteria, baselining and benchmarking the target organization's processes and people, identifying integration risks, assessing cost-and-revenue synergies, and detailing integration operating mechanisms (starting with a launch strategy and ending with granular plans by function).

2. Prevent Future Integrity Problems

Throughout this complex process, special attention is paid to embedding GE's integrity culture, systems, and processes in the acquired company. Systematic identification of gaps across all the general principles and practices discussed in section III is vital—for example, integrity infrastructure, global standards, early-warning systems, and employee "voice."

In global transactions, especially in developing nations, leaders must explicitly address two key, interrelated issues: country risk and the culture of acquired employees. They must build the corporation's special approach to emerging market issues—from payment systems to the management of remote sites to supply-chain discipline—into the due diligence/acquisition integration process. Beyond these heightened operational concerns, GE explicitly recognized in its acquisition-team guidelines that "cultural integration is one of the most underestimated complexities" in acquisitions, both to realize economic value and to embed (or supplement) a performance-with-integrity ethic.

Attending to these issues is a core responsibility of diligence and integration leaders, not just the financial, legal, and HR staffs. Specific tools—such as detailed process maps and comprehensive integrity check-lists—are key to a comprehensive risk assessments and risk-mitigation plans. More informal meetings are necessary to address cultural differences. Time is of the essence, as well. Any new problems that arise after the deal closes are increasingly likely—at least in the eyes of regulators and the media—to be attributed to the acquirer. With this in mind, it makes sense to have detailed thirty-, sixty- and one hundred–day plans on all issues, including integrity systems and processes.

3. Uncover and Address Past Problems

Uncovering the target's past problems is as important as preventing new ones after the closing. But even with the best intentions and a comprehensive due diligence approach, this remains a difficult task. Some problems may be hidden by fraud, and a number of factors may constrain diligence prior to signing: limited time, the negotiating strength of the seller, an auction setting, a public-company deal, or some combination of these factors. But addressing past problems in a timely fashion is key. This may be accomplished through:

- **Contract protections.** An issue *discovered* in diligence—for example, environmental costs running into the hundreds of millions that were ignored by the seller—can enter into the price discussion. Depending on its bargaining power, the acquirer can try to mitigate *undiscovered* adverse economic impacts of integrity issues through traditional deal techniques: representations, warranties, covenants, and indemnifications from the seller up to or after the closing (if there is a successor), as well as a "material adverse change" clause that allows the acquirer to crater the deal (or renegotiate the price) if adverse events occur after signing but before closing. Acquirers should have a toolkit of model clauses that define specific adverse developments on integrity issues discovered during the deal process (e.g., improper payments, privacy, EHS, and export controls).

- **Preclosing agreements with regulators.** If serious problems are discovered in diligence, the acquirer may want the seller to resolve both corporate and individual liability, whether criminal or civil, with the regulators before closing. In the '90s, a major company like GE—with a positive reputation for its compliance efforts—could disclose an improper payments problem to the Justice Department or the SEC and obtain an understanding that if the deal closed, the regulators would pursue individuals from the target but would not charge the acquirer criminally (and perhaps not even impose a civil fine for the target's misdeeds). More recently, though, U.S. regulators have taken the position that self-disclosure prior to closing does not necessarily lead to acquirer avoidance of corporate criminal liability—that is, "buy it, fix it" may not work even for a "good" company. Before the deal closes, the regulators may require from the target guilty pleas, disgorgement, large penalties and fines, mandated compliance systems, and even corporate monitors who will survive the closing. Buyers may thus face a stark, unpleasant choice: endure the delay and uncertainty of seller resolution with the authorities before closing; close, and inherit potential (or likely) criminal problems; or just crater the deal. For example, in one case, GE decided to wait more than a year for the target to resolve improper payment issues, rather than inherit a criminal problem. It chose to forego another deal when significant regulatory issues surfaced in due diligence prior to the closing.

- **Postclosing agreements with regulators.** In addition to preventing new problems once it has control, the acquirer must audit and investigate intensely to uncover the target's past problems that did not emerge during diligence or preclosing planning. This entails very fine-grained inquiries into a host of complex operational issues with integrity dimensions (such as "consultant" selection and payment processes, improper cash management, invalid customer discounts, and false submissions in government contracting). Again, time is of the essence. If the acquirer promptly discovers, stops, and remediates past improper practices, it can fairly argue to regulators that it did all it could reasonably be expected to do. It will be asked to explain, however, why the issue wasn't discovered during diligence and whether it should have been known earlier. If there are good answers to those questions, the acquirer may be able to negotiate a reasonable disposition that does no harm to its reputation. But if the acquirer delays in discovering and remedying these pre-existing issues, then regulators may well view them as the acquirer's problems, rather than the target's.

Crisis Management

The CEO's phone rings. The call is coming in from the CFO or maybe the GC. It's not good news.

Perhaps the SEC has opened a formal investigation into allegations of financial misstatements. Or perhaps the company has received internal reports that a small number of products (out of millions in the field) have a defect that may cause house fires. Or maybe the European regulators have conducted a dawn raid on all the offices of a major division, seeking evidence of price-fixing. Or maybe an employee has reported to the ombudsperson that regulatory documents are being falsified at the request of a major customer.

In large corporations, and in small ones, such things inevitably happen. When it was Jack Welch's or Jeff Immelt's phone that rang with the bad news, my phone rang within minutes. I'd be called down to the corner office to help form a team tasked with reacting immediately.

Crisis management is the "stress test" for companies that aim to fuse high performance with high integrity. It comes with many pitfalls. (For example: much as they'd like to, impatient CEOs cannot pick up the phone and start interviewing witnesses!) It requires a strategy on many fronts. In particular, two practices have special significance for the CEO.

1. *"It is our problem from the instant we hear about it."*

With integrity issues, it is vital that the CEO assume full responsibility from the moment he or she hears about it. If the CEO and the top leadership stall or are otherwise unresponsive, the problem—which didn't involve the top leaders in any way—becomes their problem. Delay also sends a message of indifference that will be heard both inside the company and by regulators. Inevitably, this makes a smaller issue much larger.

When these events happened at GE and were reported to senior management, we would say to each other—in the offices and hallways—We will be judged by what we do from this moment on. And it's true: the board, the regulators, and the public use the way these crises are handled to assess the character of the company's senior leaders.

As with performance crises, the CEO needs to ask the top team—often the CFO, inside auditors, and the GC—to assemble a working group with the right skills to protect documents and, within a short period of time, to answer a number of fundamental questions. For example:

- Is there a practice that must be stopped immediately, or a product withdrawn from the market without delay, to protect the public— and the company's reputation?

- What is shape and size of the problem?

- What is the next phase of the inquiry?

- Should outside experts be retained?

- Should the board be informed?

- Must the matter be disclosed to authorities under law, should it be disclosed voluntarily, or should it not be disclosed because we don't yet know enough?

- Do any employees need to be put on leave, pending completion of the inquiry?

- What types of communications should be made to constituencies inside and outside the company, ranging from employees to investors to the media?

Regular updates on all these questions are necessary, especially as new fronts open up (e.g., media stories, other regulatory actions, private suits).

Failure to jump on an integrity issue can have serious consequences for both the CEO and the company. In the spring of 2004, and then again in September, the New York attorney general informed Marsh & McLennan that his office was investigating allegations of bid rigging and unlawful conflicts of interest in the firm's role as broker between insurers and insured parties. According to news reports, the company met with the attorney general in the fall and had little to report based on any internal inquiries. This nonresponsiveness to potential criminal issues so angered the attorney general that he filed a civil bid-rigging and collusion action, announced publicly that he would no longer deal with the CEO, and threatened the company with criminal action (which, as the sad saga of the Andersen accounting firm illustrates, might well have killed the company).

The perfect storm ensued: the company's market cap sank, its credit rating was downgraded, credit dried up, sixty subpoenas were filed against the company by federal and state regulators, and a wide variety of plaintiffs brought additional suits.[4]

One can certainly fault the attorney general's public tactics of simultaneously refusing to deal with the CEO and threatening "death penalty" criminal action against the company. For its part though, MarshMac had failed, according to media reports, to respond promptly and seriously to a grave warning received months before. The company's board soon removed the CEO and the GC. The new CEO, Michael Cherkasky, negotiated a civil settlement—thereby avoiding the toxic criminal indictment—and began the long process of digging MarshMac out of the hole into which it had so suddenly fallen.[5]

Unfortunately, MarshMac was not the rare aberration. The failure to act promptly is a recurring corporate problem, with Ford/Bridgestone (tire failures), Salomon Brothers (false bidding), and Beech-Nut (adulterated apple juice) providing examples from the past twenty years of delay making a bad problem worse.[6] By contrast, more than two decades after the fact, Johnson & Johnson's immediate removal of all Tylenol products from the shelves after learning about a few poisoned bottles still serves as exhibit A for how to respond to protect public safety—and corporate reputation.[7]

2. Follow the Facts

One of the most difficult aspects of managing an integrity crisis is to allow the facts to develop in a searching, honest, and comprehensive way. There is a very human reflex to defend the company, denounce a regulator, or protect an employee who is known and liked at headquarters. Indeed, some companies always protest and defend, regardless of the facts. This may be understandable, but it's a mistake.

There is also a very human instinct on the part of the CEO to want to know quickly—sometimes at warp speed!—what has actually happened. As noted, he or she may be tempted to start questioning employees personally (also a mistake!). But as a complex organization tries to understand past events that may have happened over an extended period of time, in different locales, involving lots of players, finding the facts requires "all deliberate speed." The company must develop a very careful understanding of the facts, even if the process is disruptive or frustratingly slow. It may face the painful dilemma of not revealing all it knows—either because it will lose tactical advantage or because disclosure may antagonize regulators (even though they may be unfairly leaking to the news media).

Any facts the company discloses prior to a proceeding must be absolutely accurate. This is vital to the company's credibility with regulators, the media, employees, and other stakeholders. Sound facts are also vital to fairness in disciplining or terminating employees (and sustaining such terminations in the face of employment suits). At GE, in order to ensure fairness in individual discipline in complex cases, we tried to conduct investigations in ways that were searching and complete. On the other hand, they weren't pursued with the kind of rough prosecutorial style that might make employees feel we were presuming their guilt. Tension is not avoidable: Inspector Javert is. Often we let employees review and challenge our dossier of facts and thus make their case before sanctions were imposed.

Ultimately, when placed in the framework of particular financial or legal rules, the facts will guide (or even dictate) the company's course of action. If the facts are clearly adverse and there is little doubt about a violation, the company should, in most cases, admit the impropriety, take the steps necessary to fix the problem, and get the matter behind it. If the evidence doesn't show any corporate culpability, the company should refuse to settle or admit any wrongdoing (even though the irrationality of our legal system may ultimately lead to a nominal settlement). If the facts remain murky, then the "fight or settle" debate has to be joined at the top of the company (while promptly addressing the underlying problem, even if that problem is not clearly illegal).

As GE's general counsel, I tried to emphasize that each crisis had to be evaluated on the basis of a particular set of facts in the context of the particular financial or legal rules. There was no single "GE Way." For example, in the Israel aircraft engine case mentioned earlier, there was little question after an initial inquiry that GE employees had committed a fraud involving U.S. funds used by Israel to procure U.S. fighters (with GE engines). In addition to internal discipline and systems repair, we promptly resolved the case with the SEC and the Justice Department, even though it involved a criminal plea as well as civil fines. Jack Welch wanted a thorough cleanup of a clear-cut mess, and he led that cleanup personally. In his subsequent testimony before an aggressive congressional subcommittee, he was publicly praised—

rather than eviscerated!—for his decisive action, in contrast to many other CEOs who have been hauled before Congress (and the cameras!).

Several years after the Israeli fraud case, we chose to fight criminal price-fixing charges brought by the Department of Justice against GE's industrial diamonds business (now no longer part of the company). Here the facts were more favorable. The initial inquiry was sparked by a former head of the business who claimed he had been fired for resisting such price-fixing. But we had clear documentary evidence, including contemporaneous personal notes from Jack Welch, showing that that this individual had been fired on performance grounds. Our own investigation convinced us further that the Department of Justice did not have a case, so we made the difficult decision to take a criminal indictment. We hated seeing "above the fold" stories about criminal charges against GE, and we understood that the risk to our corporate reputation was substantial. In the resulting 1994 criminal trial in Columbus, Ohio, the federal district judge took a highly unusual action and dismissed the case against GE after the government had put in its case but before GE had completed its defense and before the case was submitted to the jury. He ruled that the government had failed to prove a key element of the offense.[8]

The facts can hurt or help your case—but they are indispensable. Develop them carefully. Follow them faithfully.

Public Policy

Governmental decisions across the globe have a major effect on industry structure, competitiveness, and profitability. The Chinese government, for example, "intervenes in every aspect of the economy."[9] But many corporations engage only in defensive, short-term, or narrowly self-interested "government relations." Fewer companies seek to make sophisticated public-policy formation and implementation an important dimension of their business's global growth—and corporate citizenship—strategies.

This is a missed opportunity. In a rapidly changing world, the possibilities for public-policy positions that advance both private and public interests are legion. They include, for example:

- Stimulating policy paradigm shifts, like putting more emphasis on early diagnosis and prevention in health care or on carbon constraints and renewable fuel sources in energy

- Working with emerging economies to help define a nation's infrastructure needs or the appropriate mix of technologies in key sectors like transportation or energy

- Working with government to obtain needed short-term support for the creation of whole new markets for public goods—like wind power, clean water, or clean coal—and for approval of new products (e.g., hybrid loco-motives) and processes (e.g., the replacement of angiography by less invasive volume CT scans)

Affirmative and strategic public-policy initiatives can advance growth and performance but must be consistent with corporate citizenship and integrity. The following three high-priority practices are a place to start.

1. Build Capacity

CEOs need to create the capacity to integrate public-policy issues inside their strategy processes and to develop sophisticated public-policy options that fairly balance company interests and public interests.[10] Capacity building must start with the commitment of the CEO and top leadership. It must be based on a sophisticated understanding of policy and political processes and on an intuitive appreciation of the difficulty and time required to move these issues in different political cultures across the globe. Not all priorities will be short term. Not all will be winners. But the cost of investing in people and ideas is tiny, compared to the potential benefits.

To build capacity, companies first have to hire experts who understand how their area of substantive policy knowledge (of tax, health care, energy, for example) intersects with business and politics. They should operate out of company headquarters on strategic business teams, rather than away from corporate action in political capitals (as the "government relations" staff does). The task of these policy experts is to understand the different trajectories of public policy and the corporation's interests and then to develop feasible policy ideas which chart a path between the status quo and the ideal—for example, policies to encourage coal gasification and carbon sequestration. As I have argued above, for crosscutting functional issues like tax, antitrust, intellectual property, environment, labor, and employment, the corporation should hire "A" players who can not only address transactional, planning, and operational issues with a firm eye on integrity, but also have public-policy capabilities on major issues like tax reform or environmental policy. At the same time, of course, it is also critical to have industry or sector "policy" experts baked into particular businesses like communications, energy, health care, transportation, and consumer finance. The key capacity-building process is to develop public-policy priorities in the annual business strategy reviews with the whole business team, rather than separate "government relations" reviews. In a nutshell, this entails systematically developing—in each major market, every year—proposed and potential policy initiatives drawing from the existing public agenda and from the company's own ideas. These market-by-market analyses then need to be aggregated and integrated in the annual business strategy review to establish global priorities (not all issues can be pursued), according to a combination of value to the company, benefit to society, and political feasibility. With different electricity-producing technologies (steam, gas, combined cycle, nuclear, wind, solar), with operations all across the globe, and with heavy government involvement in the issue, GE Energy used this bottom-up policy process most effectively to set global policy priorities in its core strategy review with the CEO. In a complementary process, GE China seeks to prioritize in-country issues arising from the company's different businesses.[11]

2. Focus on Credible Policy, Avoiding Partisanship and Corruption

Clearly, proactive corporate forays into public policy raise the risks inherent in political action: harsh criticism, attacks on motives, and distorted media accounts. So the corporation that seeks active engagement in public policy—while still maintaining its reputation for high integrity—has to establish and observe certain guidelines:

- **The process of implementing policy in the political arena must be conducted by political professionals in** *local* **seats of power (usually, national or state capitals) who mirror the policy professionals developing policy in headquarters.** These political professionals have a sophisticated understanding of the nation's political culture, they understand business, they understand the policy, and they have high integrity in developing relationships with the "customers", the key governmental leaders. They don't bribe, for starters. Finding these high-integrity political and policy professionals is relatively easy in the United States and the EU; it's much harder elsewhere.

- **The policies must be balanced.** In this age of
  instant communication and widespread distrust of corporations, disingenuous posturing
  will be exposed as such, and quickly. Special
  provisions designed to line the company's
  pockets are inherently troublesome. Policy
  prescriptions must recognize that most public
  debates involve values in conflict, such as the
  classic equity-versus-efficiency arguments
  about regulation or the basic tensions between
  cost, quality, and access in health-care policy.
  Explicitly acknowledging these tensions—and
  trying to articulate a fair balance between
  legitimate competing concerns—is necessary if
  the proposal is to be credible and command
  respect.

  The company must pay scrupulous
  attention to the accuracy of facts—and the
  basic credibility of factual assumptions—upon
  which a proposed policy is based. Using experts
  with outstanding reputations outside of corporate consulting—and fully disclosing any
  financial arrangements when questioned—
  will not stop disputes about key facts or
  fundamental factual assumptions but will help
  demonstrate openness and good faith.

- **The twin goals should be bipartisan solutions and a nonpartisan stance.** Partisan politics may help a company in the short run. But in politics, the pendulum eventually swings in the opposite direction, and the partisan corporation gets hurt. Especially in a bitterly partisan era in the United States, unwavering support for substantive principles serves companies better than unbalanced support for political parties. People can understand and respect well-thought-out positions, even if they disagree.

- **Emphasizing substantive policy positions is even more important in emerging markets,** where it can be dangerous for a company to be too closely associated with the personalities and politics of a particular regime. In those nations, the pendulum can swing even more wildly, with disastrous results for a politicized transnational company.

3. Make the Connection Between Public Policy and Corporate Citizenship

At GE, we tried to orient our public-policy approach toward all three elements of corporate citizenship: (1) strong, sustained economic performance, (2) adherence to formal financial and legal rules, and (3) ethical actions beyond formal requirements.

With respect to strong, sustained commercial performance, many in business, academia, and the NGO community are calling on corporations to solve some of the world's most pressing problems—for example, lack of health care, inadequate housing, shortages of clean water, skyrocketing energy prices, and climate change. The goal is to bring these demands into congruence with durable for-profit commercial activity.[12] GE now projects that much of its future growth will come from meeting the infrastructure needs of developing nations.[13] It unabashedly called ecomagination—the corporate effort to produce environmentally friendly technologies—a business initiative, captured in the shorthand phrase "Green is green."

The ecomagination initiative also provides an example of the huge public-policy issues that may lurk behind, and dictate the timing of, a commercial effort. When the initiative was announced in May 2005, there was a bitter partisan debate raging in Washington on climate change—a debate that was going nowhere. The company purposefully steered clear of specific public-policy proposals at that time (although it did talk in very general terms about the need to live in a carbon-constrained world). GE wanted to emphasize a change in commercial strategy, not fall into the bubbling vat of policy controversy. By 2007, however—due in part to GE's role in helping to mainstream the climate change issue in the corporate community—the company felt that the time was right to seek out industrial and environmental allies and propose specific policies on climate change that would involve a combination of legal requirements (e.g., a cap on carbon emissions) and market mechanisms (e.g., trading carbon credits).

Robust adherence to formal legal and financial rules that do exist is the second pillar of corporate citizenship. Yet there is a never-ending policy debate about whether some of those rules *should* exist (at least in their current form). When engaging in such debates, corporations need to exhibit the balance and credibility discussed just above. At times, though, there is the need not to modify rules, but to extend them, in order to improve fairness, enhance competition, and reduce cost.

A salient example is the effort by some American corporations to extend the U.S. prohibitions against corporate bribery of foreign officials, especially in developing markets, to corporations based in other industrialized nations. Because public official bribery, extortion, and misappropriation are a cancer inside companies, impede state building, retard economic development, and distort competition by imposing illicit costs, these U.S. companies helped form the world's leading anticorruption NGO, Transparency International. They pushed for an OECD Convention that was adopted in the late 1990s, with thirty-four industrialized nations agreeing to make foreign bribery a crime under their national laws. Rather than "level down" U.S. law, U.S. companies successfully sought to "level up" the laws of other nations.[14]

The third pillar of citizenship, as noted above, involves voluntarily making ethical commitments beyond the formal requirements that bind a company. But such standards come with costs. For example, GE voluntarily embraced "ethical" sourcing, regardless of whether its competitors did so. It concluded that the benefits of such a move were sufficient, in part because it had to evaluate suppliers one by one on quality and viability anyway.

Clearly, in a competitive world, there are limits to this kind of unilateral action. It's very unlikely, for example, that any company would take on the enormous cost of remediating historic environmental problems—which often resulted from actions lawful at the time—unless all similarly situated corporations did so, as well. So in contemplating "ethical" actions, companies may decide that a particular "public" or "social good" is important to society (such as environmental protection), but conclude that the competitive impact is too great to go it alone. In such cases, the costs must be more broadly distributed, usually in one of two ways:

- Through voluntary, industrywide agreement on standards (promulgated, of course, in ways that don't violate the competition laws)

- Through public policy, where costs are spread either by means of the tax base or through imposition of costs or responsibilities on all members of a particular industry

This debate often plays itself out very publicly. In the fall of 2007, for example, American toy makers facing product safety issues on China imports—including the use of lead paint that was specifically prohibited by their specs—were debating whether to improve company supplier standards, voluntarily establish industrywide testing mechanisms, or seek legislative action from Washington.[15]

When corporate responsibility advocates fail to get their way in legislatures, they may shift focus and ask corporations individually to bear costs that are true "social" costs—in other words, costs that society or business sectors as a whole should bear. This is well intentioned but misguided. If the issue involves an important "social good," the best competitive solution may be public policy that levels the playing field for concerned corporations and free riders alike and is also enforceable (which voluntary action or industry agreements are not).

Thus, in both the developed and the developing worlds, corporations should consider legislative regimes in such core areas as health care, environmental health and safety, consumer finance, and drug safety. Of course, a sound approach is needed, combining mandates with market mechanisms to keep competitiveness high and inflation low where possible. This may sound like heresy to some in the business world, but I believe it is the fairest and most competitive approach if the issue is important to society and—by building a stronger society—to business.

Reputation

A corporation's reputation may be hard to quantify, but it is of surpassing importance. As a recent *Harvard Business Review* article put it, "Executives know the importance of their companies' reputation . . . in an economy where 70% to 80% of market value comes from hard-to-assess intangible assets such as brand equity, intellectual capital and goodwill, organizations are especially vulnerable to anything that damages their reputations."[16]

Although performance is the core of a company's reputation, so is its integrity—and the integrity of its CEO.[17] It's an oft-repeated truism—but it's still true—that reputation, like a forest, takes years to grow but can burn down overnight. At GE, we took this caution to heart because we knew that our size and our generally good reputation, built up over many years, made us a constant target and that any misstep on our part would be magnified.

The following four precepts, which flow out of my previous points, are at the core of building and sustaining a reputation for integrity.

1. Keep Commitments

Although "reputation" is in a sense *perception*—the collective impression of widely diverse constituencies, each with specific interests and concerns—an enduring reputation is in fact built on reality: on sustained implementation of the core integrity practices and principles, with as few misses as possible. It is really that fundamental, and few words are required to make the point. It's also built on the reality of what happens when misses do occur. As noted earlier, skillful crisis management can contain the reputational damage, or even enhance the reputation of a company that promptly, candidly, and effectively remedies a serious problem.

2. Anticipate the Issues

A second important component of a reputation for integrity is anticipating and responding to emerging issues. A going-forward strategy starts with different approaches to different stakeholders, and it builds on the constituency-assessment processes discussed above for determining global standards and for obtaining early warnings. The CEO needs to structure those stakeholder-by-stakeholder processes—and specific communication strategies—through existing direct reports who have day-to-day responsibility.[18] (At GE, for example, these would have included the head of NBC, the president of GE Energy, the head of GE environmental programs, and the company HR leader, among others.)

These strategies may require more listening and better communication one-on-one—focused both on explaining company positions *and* on showing sensitivity to stakeholder concerns. They may involve public positioning to help shape a debate or demonstrate a broad understanding on an emerging issue— climate change, health-care costs, the safety of products sourced from abroad, the effect of globalization on the U.S. labor force—without taking a precise public position. They may involve analyses of where trends are going and also identifying issues that are not of immediate importance but may become so.

As the company decides whether or not to take specific action, the core of the decision must be the merits—the cost-benefit analysis of what is in the company's long-term enlightened self-interest. It is neither possible nor desirable to appease every stakeholder group or blindly sign on to every NGO's proposed code of conduct. A good reputation with a stakeholder group is part of the calculus, but the proposed action must make sense on other substantive grounds. GE said no far more often to stakeholder requests than we said yes—although when we said no, we tried to do so with respect.

From this bottom-up stakeholder process will also emerge broad corporate themes beyond narrow constituency interests, which the CEO can tap for investor-relations efforts, advertising, or other major corporate public communications. What is the company's position on globalization, health-care costs, environmental protection, or consumer protection? Aggregating, centralizing, and synthesizing companywide reputation themes helps keep reputational analysis and decisions rooted in the realities of the company, the marketplace, and society. It also highlights the inevitable instances in which stakeholder interests conflict—as in a huge subject like globalization—and helps develop communications that address those differences (e.g., reduction in U.S. jobs versus development of a competitive cost structure).

3. Generate a Substantive Citizenship Report

The annual report provides extensive detail on performance. A substantive citizenship report provides comparable detail on integrity.

There is now a vast industry that rates companies on reputation, integrity, citizenship, and other nonfinancial criteria. These ratings are based on surveys or company data and are aimed at either the general public or more specific constituencies. As a rule, GE considered positive ratings from these third-party entities to be valuable in burnishing its general reputation. (Since 2000, GE has consistently been at the top of *Fortune*'s "most admired" and the *Financial Times'* "most respected" list of global companies; more recently, the company qualified for the competitive Dow Jones Sustainability Index.)

At the same time, we knew that, for most people, the methodology behind the ratings relating to both performance and integrity was opaque, and the summary conclusions associated with these kinds of rankings didn't come close to revealing the extent of our integrity efforts.[19] To address this issue, GE in 2005 issued its first "citizenship report" as a complement to the company's management discussion and analysis in the annual report.

Of course, GE was not alone in taking this step. Many companies in this same time period began issuing some kind of citizenship or sustainability report. Truth be told, some of these were long on pictures and short on detail. For its part, GE saw this new report as an opportunity to report in detail on the company's integrity systems, processes, results, issues, and future actions.

But how could the report be shaped so that it would be something more than just self-serving puffery? After much internal discussion, GE laid out the report's structure and issues following a template developed by a well-respected nonprofit—the Global Reporting Initiative—which is increasingly used by multinational corporations to present systematically a sequence of issues of concern to global stakeholders.[20] The report provides links to GE's integrity Web site, so readers can review the relevant GE policies and guidelines in their entirety. It presents hard facts that allow for year-over-year comparisons in specific areas, including, for example:

- Issues reported and resolved through the ombuds system

- Employee diversity and survey results

- The number of suppliers reviewed (and terminated)

- Money spent on education and training

- Companywide EHS data (spills, releases, individuals trained, results of agency inspections)

It also includes controversial issues—for example, GE as a proponent of nuclear power, the company's role in stem cell research, the corporate perspective on TV program content, wages in emerging markets, and efforts to address nascent legal and ethical concerns arising from nanotechnology. At the same time, it candidly addresses embarrassing integrity lapses. For example, the 2007 report described a consent decree with the FDA that temporarily closed down a unit of GE Healthcare (Jeff Immelt's former business) for missing quality standards.

The annual citizenship report is a moving target. GE regularly holds meetings with activist stakeholders in the United States and abroad to discuss the scope and shape of the report. It has made changes in more recent editions—including more emphasis on financial-services issues and the inclusion of more forward-looking targets—as a result of those discussions.

4. Communicate Reality to Create Perception

A strong reputation, as noted, is built on the foundation of a strong reality. But it is also built on the statements that describe that reality. Are the corporation's statements fully accurate? Are the actions promised being fully implemented in good faith? Whether it is a communication to an investor about the future growth areas of the company, or to an NGO about global sourcing, or to all constituencies in the citizenship report, credibility is all.

With this caution in mind, GE spent more than a year planning its ecomagination initiative. Also in mind was the significant hit that Ford's reputation and credibility took when it had to abandon its promise of a more fuel-efficient SUV: the victim of unanticipated technology and cost constraints. The ecomagination initiative was viewed internally as a significant business and reputational opportunity, but also as one with a huge downside if GE failed.

Ecomagination caught people's attention because it was about a sexy topic—climate change—but also because it was about substance, which could be measured. It was based on seventeen technologies that were already in the market and had proven operational and environmental improvements over prior products. Second, ecomagination included "vision within boundaries." In other words, it promised precise amounts of new R&D spending and predicted the introduction of additional technologies that could meet "stretch" environmental and operational criteria. And finally, it committed to an absolute reduction in company greenhouse gas emissions and to an increase in internal energy efficiency. These internal efforts would be a "proof statement" that the technologies worked.

The launch of comagination clearly enhanced GE's reputation. But these reputational gains could only be sustained if GE fairly reported on its progress—and if it met its commitments. Reputation, in the end, would turn not on a popular "eco" ad—an elephant dancing to "Singin' in the Rain"—but on the credibility of GE's claims and of its reports on those claims.[22]

V. The Right-Sized Role of the Board

Although only the CEO can achieve the fusion of high performance with high integrity, the board of directors also plays a vital role in helping—and ensuring that—the CEO and top company leaders carry out this fundamental task.

Due to Sarbanes-Oxley and other post-Enron reforms, we hear recurring lamentations that board members focus more on "compliance" than "strategy." But the vital board role I'm advocating does not require directors to engage in an endless review of compliance minutiae to cover their posteriors— nor does it compel CEOs to shovel mind-numbing detail at the board to cover *theirs*. Instead, the board's contribution to high performance with high integrity grows directly out of its basic oversight of corporate strategy, properly defined.

I attended every GE board and audit committee meeting between 1987 and 2005. On the basis of that experience, I am convinced that the board can assess whether the CEO and company leaders are creating an effective performance-with-integrity culture in the same way that it assesses other strategic fundamentals—that is, at an appropriate, but not excruciating, level of detail. For their part, CEOs need to build credibility and trust with the board regarding their intensity, commitment—and effectiveness. Such trust is crucial when the ill winds of impropriety blow through some corner of the organization, as they inevitably will. Then the board will need (demand!) far more detail and spend far more of its time on the problem—and the CEO may need directors to stand up for the company.

Such problems deflect the board from more affirmative pursuits, just as they demand inordinate amounts of CEO time. That is why overseeing the creation of a high-performance-with-high-integrity culture—and implementation of the key principles and practices described previously—is so important. It focuses the board on the right front-end questions, minimizes the flow of out-of-context minutiae, and helps avoid the kinds of back-end problems that do require inordinate detail and director time.

The first step, of course, is getting the right CEO.

A New Spec for the CEO

When a board begins to address its most important responsibility—CEO succession—it's certain to ask itself whether the leading candidates for the job have business vision and leadership skills. It's almost as certain to ask whether those candidates are individuals of high personal integrity. Are they honest and candid? Do they keep their word? Are they fair-minded?

But boards have to go further. They need to ask whether the candidate at hand has a deep cultural and organizational commitment to fuse high performance with high integrity. Does he or she have the necessary experience, knowledge, and skills—both as a leader and as a manager—to carry out this critical task of fusion in a challenging, fast-changing, and unforgiving environment? In short, the board has to add a new specification to the CEO's job description and then find a person who meets that "spec." So, too, the management development process—led by the CEO and overseen by the board—needs to focus on this performance with integrity spec for high-potential individuals promoted into top P&L jobs and business division leadership.[1]

This performance-with-integrity spec for CEOs has been central in recent forced-succession situations. Michael Cherkasky, the head of Marsh &

McLennan's private investigative arm, was chosen to succeed Jeffrey Greenberg when it became clear that the very survival of the firm depended on, first, successful negotiations with regulators and, second, the development of integrity systems, processes, and—ultimately—culture.

Boards also have gone outside to find suitable successors to present to the world a person unburdened by the company's past. Boeing chose Jim McNerney of 3M after procurement, conflict-of-interest, and personal scandals had taken down two CEOs and a CFO. Siemens hired Peter Löscher of Merck after the chair of the supervisory board resigned and the CEO's contract was not renewed, amid the burgeoning overseas bribery scandal referred to earlier.

Building high performance with high integrity into the job description, and spotlighting it in the management development and CEO succession processes, is far better than trying to deal with this foundational leadership issue after the house catches fire.

Strategy and Board Oversight: Taking the Broad View

In complex corporations, the board should define strategy broadly. That definition should comprise not just the company's commercial strategy, but also its approach to its highest-priority risks and opportunities in the near, middle, and long term.

By embracing this broad definition, the board necessarily pays special attention to the CEO's approach to performance with integrity. It focuses on both systemic challenges and "one-off" issues of the highest priority. Because it is simply impossible in the time available for the board to review more than first-order issues, setting the board's agenda effectively defines the issues composing company strategy.

When the GE board rewrote the company's governance precepts in 2002, it required that the board and the CEO together determine at the end of one year the key risks and opportunities facing the company in the year ahead. Those issues then became the core board agenda and were addressed in depth at board and committee meetings scheduled systematically across the subsequent calendar year. High-level performance-with-integrity issues have an important place on these board and committee calendars. The basic principles and practices discussed above should be covered on a recurring basis. Specific agenda items might include the audit staff's proposed work plan, the integrity dimensions of deals, environmental health and safety risk abatement, dealing with emerging market risk in China (or the Middle East or Indonesia), and the response to high-visibility, high-impact controversies. The regular meetings of the nonmanagement directors—one of the best governance reforms, post-Enron—can add integrity issues to these agendas as events unfold. The board's decisions about strategy should involve a review of both the substance of management decisions and the processes for making those decisions within the company. The board's fundamental role throughout should be one of constructive criticism. It should seek relevant information and ask hard questions, in an effort to ensure that there was a reasonable process that led to a solid substantive position within a reasonable range of management discretion.

The board does not customarily substitute its judgment for that of management. In overseeing the performance-with-integrity strategy, therefore, the board does not need to master minutiae or design the program. But it must take most seriously questions about whether the articulated aspirations, financial incentives, and potential penalties create an integrity culture, and whether key principles and practices—including rigorous systems and processes—are being implemented by business leaders.

The right level of information for board decisions and oversight may vary, including either advance materials of varying depth, or briefings at the meetings, or both. But the goal should always be the same: the

CEO and top leaders must communicate with the utmost candor on the company's opportunities, risks, options, and hardest trade-offs. Exposing, not hiding, the critical dimensions of difficult decisions or complex systems allows the board to ask good questions—on the basis of its own relevant experience—about management's proposed action, and helps it avoid getting lost in the detail.

In other words, it's the quality of information, the honest essence of the matter, not the quantity, that is vital to the board's strategic oversight role. For complex deals involving significant integrity risk, and for complex regulatory matters with significant financial and reputational risk, analyzing and debating an issue for several meetings prior to decision can be far more effective than a one-meeting blitz based on phone book–sized briefing papers.

Key Indicators

How, then, can the board know that the company is fusing high performance with high integrity? Again, the answer starts with the CEO, who needs to define the type of information that can be tracked over time to answer this core assessment question. The board then has to approve and "own" those key metrics, which might include the following.

1. *General Indicators*

The integrity metrics used to assess management performance described earlier can be adapted for summary presentation to the board, and could include the following:

- The reviews by the corporate audit staff and the outside auditors of controllership and integrity policy issues, with special reports from the auditors, the CFO, or the GC on persistent or serious problems in particular businesses and geographies

- Reports from the company's corporate compliance review board on each business's integrity program

- Special in-depth reports from functional experts at corporate headquarters who are responsible for the company's overall approach to critical issues: environment, health and safety, sourcing, SEC issues, and labor and employment, among others

- Review of concerns bubbling up in the company's ombuds system and the directors' own hotline: how many reports by policy, business, and geography; how many serious policy violations; how many open matters; how long on average to close them out; and key trends—and implications for action—from all these data points

- An assessment of the trends by business, policy, and geography in formal government proceedings (defined as either actual cases brought by the government or formal investigations involving subpoenas), in informal governmental inquiries, and in private lawsuits

- An assessment of whether the early-warning systems are working by determining whether key controversies or problems were anticipated by the company—and if not, *why* not?

- A review of the integrity questions in employee surveys across businesses—not just for the company as a whole, but by division and unit

These indicators can be reviewed annually and systematically, some in the audit (or other) committee context and some at the full board level. In all cases, they should be reviewed on a trend-line basis, comparing year over year.

2. Specific Indicators

Board member visits to the businesses without se-nior management in attendance allow hard, direct questioning of business leaders on key performance and integrity issues. (GE requires its directors to make at least two such visits a year.) In addition, the board needs in-depth understanding of the com-pany's significant misses: a financial restatement, a bribery case, a failure to follow ethical sourcing stan-dards, a consumer finance class-action suit that had to be settled, and similar problems. The particulars of each matter must be explained in a concise, com-prehensive way on an ongoing basis.

At the same time, the CEO and the top leadership also need to discuss root causes and remedies. Spe-cific events can almost always serve as important windows on system failures and needed improve-ments, and the CEO should make sure that the board can see clearly through the particular event to the larger questions. The Israeli Aircraft Engine scandal at GE, for example, led not only to detailed company inquiry into the specific offense, but also to a broader analysis of how to fix underlying processes relating to aircraft engine sales to foreign govern-ments that were financed with U.S. funds.

3. CEO Credibility

The board has a right to expect that the CEO will not hide the ball—that he or she will be unstinting in root-cause analysis, fair-minded in self-criticism, and rigorous in proposing solutions when general indicators are trending the wrong way or when the corporation and its people have made mistakes. Board trust is based on CEO candor, especially on these sensitive issues. Jack Welch got the board's attention when he began one discussion by announcing, "Well, we totally booted *this* one!"

CEO Pay for Performance—*with Integrity*

Compensation committees may mention "integrity of the CEO" in their annual proxy statement report on executive pay. But it's the rare company that can point to a systematic process to achieve this end—one that goes beyond impressions and that establishes and then articulates a specific performance-with-integrity compensation framework for the CEO and top leaders.

Working with a new type of compensation consultant, the board and the CEO should design a compensation system that builds explicitly on the principles, practices, and key indicators discussed above. Each year, the board should evaluate:

- Specific CEO goals and objectives

- Implementation of the high-performance-with-high-integrity strategy on its own terms

- Comparisons with other peer companies (or, in the case of a large transnational like GE, with peer companies for each of its major divisions)

It should tie some proportion of base and bonus compensation to those integrity measurements and make a qualitative judgment about the CEO's success (or lack of success) on this foundational issue.

Let me stress the point. Other than the succession decision itself, no action by the board more effectively demonstrates its commitment to a high-performance-with-high-integrity culture than embedding performance with integrity in compensation decisions for the CEO and top company leaders. And through an explicit discussion of this issue in the corporation's public documents—including the proxy statement and the citizenship report—the board declares itself to the world on the importance that the company places on fusing high performance with high integrity.

This is far more than just "spin" or public relations. This is the board taking a public stand and embracing standards that it can and should be held to. CEO compensation is still a white-hot issue, and the public is looking for leadership. Setting "pay for performance *with integrity*" is an important board and CEO obligation—but also a significant opportunity.[2]

Meeting Alone with the CFO and the GC

A final thought on the board's role in overseeing a high-performance-with-high-integrity culture: the whole board—or, alternatively, the members of the audit committee—should periodically meet alone with the chief financial officer and the general counsel. The goal should be to ask uninhibited questions and receive uninhibited answers. Such meetings not only give the board multiple perspectives on the corporation; they also encourage these key staff leaders to play their all-important "guardian" role.

This can only work with a self-confident CEO, who believes that it's OK for the board to understand that the company is not perfect. If the CEO wants some idea of what the CFO or the GC plans to discuss at a separate board session, he or she may be more likely to solicit "guardian" views in the regular course of business.[3]

VI. Building the Foundation

The most important argument in this short book is that the CEOs need to own—or reclaim—the fundamental business challenge of high performance with high integrity.

Governance on the Front Lines

Throughout the preceding pages, I've tried to highlight the critical role that the CEO and other senior leaders must play in driving this issue deep into the company's business operations. In the post-Enron era, much of the governance debate about corporate performance with integrity focused on the role of the board. And although the board has a vital oversight role, I have argued that the directors simply cannot provide the sustained, rigorous, disciplined, aspirational leadership that's needed, especially in a complex, transnational company. Only the CEO can create both a relentless drive for performance and an unyielding culture of integrity—a culture that constrains pressures for corruption across and down into a company, and that inspires people to do things right and to do the right thing. We can't simply pile more and more responsibility on the board and think we are dealing with the essential leadership and management challenges from the CEO on down.

I deeply believe, therefore, that the governance debate about corporate performance with integrity must shift and focus primarily (although not exclusively) on the "third dimension" of governance: the role of the CEO and top leadership in governing the company and driving the principles and practices necessary to fuse the twin goals of capitalism. Neither the shareholders (the first dimension) nor the board (the second dimension) can do it.

As in so many other areas, CEOs must lead not just inside their companies but also outside to shape the larger debate—calling in public forums for disciplined business management and for inspirational business leadership fused in such a way to deliver high performance with high integrity. They need to discuss the hard issues, the trade-offs, and the failures, as well as the benefits and the successes. Of course, they should speak publicly about the enormous challenges of a global economy, innovative technologies, regulations in need of reform, the importance of improving our educational system. But they should also be visible and vocal about this fundamental issue at the core of capitalism—in speeches at the Business Council, the National Press Club, the economic clubs of the great cities, and forums in their communities and around the world.

By so doing, perhaps they can help shift the focus of the now increasingly sterile governance debate—which today looks almost exclusively at the board—to the complex, protean subject of CEO governance on the front lines. Perhaps they and the directors can help redefine the role the board can play in overseeing and supporting such effective governance in the company (not leading or managing it), including a new spec for the CEO and pay not just for performance but for performance *with* integrity.

Performance with Integrity: The Benefits of Corporate Citizenship

"Corporate citizenship"—or corporate social responsibility (CSR)—continues to be the subject of acrimonious and heated debate. The committed advocates of CSR argue with great passion that corporations must do more to change the world for the better and create benefits for the company's diverse stakeholders, often ignoring the impact on corporate performance. The harshest critics of CSR contend, with equal passion, that "the business of business is business," and that corporations exist principally (or only) to maximize shareholder wealth, ignoring the importance of other stakeholders to the economic well-being of the company. In isolation, neither side is right.

As described above, corporate citizenship has three interrelated dimensions: strong, sustained economic performance; rigorous compliance with the spirit and letter of formal financial and legal requirements; and global standards and integrity values beyond those formal requirements that, in the judgment of the corporate leaders, advance the reputation and long-term health of the enterprise.

High performance with high integrity is at the core of this view of corporate citizenship—and the fusion of these two fundamental goals is where the corporate citizenship debate should take place.

Strong, sustained economic performance provides dramatic benefits to all stakeholders of a corporation, and performance failures can devastate stakeholder interests. But all too often, as I've argued, this fundamental aspect of business (and the first element of citizenship) is improperly ignored or downplayed by advocates of CSR or corporate citizenship.

Equally, advocates of corporate citizenship all too often downplay corporate adherence to formal financial and legal requirements, on the grounds that this is something companies are bound to do anyway, and therefore can be taken as a given. But as I've also tried to demonstrate, such adherence requires inspired leadership and disciplined management, as well as significant expenditure of time, effort, and resources. It is worth reiterating that the consequences of significant integrity failures (like significant performance failures) can have devastating impacts on the very stakeholders whom CSR advocates claim to be representing.

On the other hand, the critics of corporate citizenship misconceive the purpose of the corporation when they argue for a simple maximization (often short-term maximization) of shareholder value. They overlook the importance to the company's long-term commercial success of going beyond narrow formal rules and behaving fairly and responsibly toward those upon whom the company relies—recruits, employees, retirees, shareholders, creditors, customers, suppliers, and communities. This can take the form of companywide global standards which corporations choose voluntarily to take every day and which create a set of internal precepts requiring strict employee adherence. This ethical dimension also involves employee commitment to the integrity values of honesty, candor, fairness, reliability and trustworthiness. Together, they create value that is the foundation for strong economic performance over the long term.

The choice is not a stark one between shareholders and other stakeholders. The task is exercising judgment on how to optimize the benefits to all whom the corporation impacts—and upon whom the corporation depends.

In exercising that judgment, the kinds of benefits that can accrue to different stakeholders from high commercial performance are well understood: growth, creditworthiness, innovation, jobs, market value, all flowing from provision of outstanding goods and services. The types of benefits that flow from high integrity—from the consistent efforts of employees who not only follow the formal and ethical rules, but also embody the personal values of honesty, fairness, candor, trustworthiness, and reliability—may be less obvious, but they are many and profound.

Inside the company, the benefits from high integrity include:

- Providing transparent processes that promote employee understanding and buy-in

- Empowering employees, both through mechanisms like business work-outs—which challenge managers' conventional wisdom—

and through mechanisms that give them "voice" on financial, legal, ethical, and reputational concerns

- Helping to connect personal values and company values, and thereby creating an all-important convergence between who people *are* and what they *do*

- Supporting an HR system based on merit, rather than cronyism or corruption

- Creating pride in the corporation

- Helping to recruit, retain, and motivate outstanding employees

- Providing a positive environment and culture for people to provide high-quality goods and services with high productivity for a company about which they care

Outside the company, in the marketplace, performance with integrity avoids (or dramatically reduces the risk of) catastrophic events—and reduces the likelihood of other significant costs, such as customer lawsuits or customer complaints or remedial environmental costs. Put more positively, the benefits of performance with integrity include:

- Contributing materially to the integrity of products and services

- Reducing the cost and increasing the effectiveness of many business processes—for example, acquisition due diligence and integration, or streamlining manufacturing, in part to reduce pollution

- Enhancing the brand

- Making the corporation a desirable partner for both customers and suppliers—and earning their trust

- Differentiating the corporation from less scrupulous competitors, and thereby creating an appeal for buyers in emerging markets who are concerned about their own reputations for integrity

- Enhancing the company's reputation in the eyes of the shareholders, creditors, and rating agencies that (for economic reasons) have added integrity risk to their investment analysis

- Appealing to the small but growing community of socially responsible investors

- Addressing emerging societal problems, like climate change, in ways that are good for both business and reputation

Finally, a corporate emphasis on integrity creates significant benefits in the broader global community, including:

- Giving the company credibility in public debates, which can help make formal rules more balanced and sensible

- Creating credibility with regulators and enforcers, which, at a minimum, can create a respectful collaborative relationship for resolving regulatory or investigative issues and, at best, can help shape remedies when problems arise

- Increasing the chances of positive media coverage, which can affect reputation and brand

- Helping restore and sustain trust in business and serving as a needed antidote to the incessant flow of negative publicity about business

- Contributing to legitimate, durable growth—even institution building—in emerging markets, which, if successful, makes those nations

stronger and a better place in which to do
business

Fusing the benefits of performance with the benefits
of integrity—on quality, employee loyalty, productivity,
customer retention, public credibility, trust in busi-
nesss—can create a potent business organization that
earns the trust of both shareholders and other stakeholders—one that is truly a good corporate citizen.

The Issue of Cost

A fundamental question remains: how much does all
this cost? Implementing the high-performance-with-
high-integrity principles and practices—and realizing
the associated benefits—isn't free. So how should we
think about costs—and whether the benefits justify
them?

Answering this question is not simple or easy, but
it's helpful to begin by looking at three distinct kinds
of costs and understanding them as investments with
the kinds of paybacks (benefits) described above.

1. The Cost of Adhering to Formal
Financial and Legal Requirements

Obviously, companies incur some cost as they seek
to comply with formal rules—which, of course, they

must do because corporations, like citizens, are not above the law. The question is one of depth, degree, energy, and investment. Should a company create systems and processes, and checks and balances, that accomplish a bare-minimum level of compliance? Or should it attempt to address both the spirit and the letter of those formal rules? Invoking an automotive metaphor, should it set out to build a MINI or a BMW 7 Series? If new people are needed to achieve compliance, should they be narrow (read "inexpensive") process controllers, or should the specialists in these areas—tax, environment, export controls, or employment—be more expensive "A" players, who are capable of major contributions in strategy, deals, public policy, as well as in navigating regulatory shoals?

In thinking about investments in the systems and processes for adhering to formal rules, it is important to remember that this particular cost can actually avoid or reduce costs elsewhere, in at least two ways. First, this investment can not only help avoid the extraordinary costs of a catastrophic integrity miss, but it can also prevent and reduce many other types of more regular costs that have a large cumulative effect: customer complaints, consumer lawsuits, employee actions, regulatory inquiries, and less catastrophic enforcement actions that, nonetheless, interrupt production or supply chains.

Second, integrity systems and processes can improve business processes, which in turn reduces costs, raises quality, speeds throughput, and achieves other good commercial ends. Risk assessment and early-warning systems on integrity issues should be an integral , complementary part of a broader assessment and mitigation of business risks. When those processes are linked to formal quality processes, it can lead to simplification and cost reduction. Integrity disciplines in deals reduce the chances that the pro formas will blow up. The energetic embrace of particular regulations can be helpful, rather than harmful: GE concluded, for example, that the requirements of Sarbanes-Oxley Section 404 actually improved its financial disciplines (in areas like revenue recognition or derivatives accounting or inventory valuation). "Front of the pipe" methods of reducing pollution under regulatory regimes can result in simpler and less costly manufacturing processes with multiple benefits.[1] Sustainable performance is a combination of entrepreneurship and discipline. I don't believe people at GE felt that the disciplines of a performance-with-integrity culture stifled sustainable innovation—quite the contrary—though it surely requires effort.

In the end, CEOs must personally decide how much to invest in integrity systems and processes aimed at adhering to formal financial and legal requirements—

weighing the degree of risk the corporation is willing to take against the offsetting benefits of costs avoided and business processes improved. Some investment is required, or the CEO or the company could face criminal charges. A company can take a minimalist approach and thereby take significant risks: investing as little as possible to create and maintain bare-bones systems and processes. A company committed to high performance with high integrity will choose to make a serious investment in robust adherence to both the spirit and the letter of financial and legal rules. Sound analysis can show CEOs the options— can assess how a given level of "cost" in adhering to rules may be a good investment from either a financial or a commonsense perspective.

2. The Cost of Adhering to Voluntarily Adopted Global Standards

As I suggested in section III, the same sort of risk-reward analysis applies when the CEO, senior management, and the board explore whether or not to adopt a global standard or commitment beyond the formal rules that bind the company and its employees.

In some cases, cost is simply not a consideration. For example, adopting a global standard of nondiscrimination in employment decisions is an imperative in a diverse, transnational company. In other instances, cost considerations definitely play a role in the search for a balanced response to a challenge. GE's ethical sourcing initiative, for example, rests on a detailed set of guidelines that must be followed when the company is qualifying suppliers. Because of practicality and resource constraints, however, the supplier inquiry, either at qualification or in contract implementation, is not as detailed as deal-related due diligence or a full-scale audit—and second- and third-tier suppliers may not be subjected to the same degree of scrutiny as first-tier suppliers.

At the far end of the spectrum, there are cases in which the exceedingly high costs of taking an action that is arguably good for business, for society, and for the economy of a nation—consumer finance protections, for example, or greenhouse gas restraints—are so enormous that public policy interventions, which apply to all competitors may be the only way to fairly distribute those costs and keep a level competitive playing field.

But as I have emphasized, decisions about global standards must measure benefits over time not only by financial analysis, but also by commonsense, real-world judgment when (as will often be the case) quantification can't capture reality.

3. The Cost of Lost Business

A third cost—the cost of business lost from performing with integrity—again is hard to measure. The most recurring issue is demands for bribes from corrupt public officials in developing nations, which prompts a predictable message from the field: if I don't pay the bribe, I don't get the business.

But here it's worth restating three profound benefits that—at least in the eyes of GE's leaders—significantly outweighed any cost of lost business. First, and most important, bribes compromise a uniform, global integrity culture; send hopelessly confusing messages; and inevitably corrupt the organization. The core employee values of honesty, candor, fairness, reliability, and trustworthiness simply can't flourish when laws are broken and the company's global standards are compromised in order to get business.

Second, bribes create significant legal, reputational, and political risk—from legal prosecution in the developed world to political attacks in the developing world when the political pendulum swings and strikes companies, which bribed the *ancient régime*. The scandal engulfing Siemens for systematic, improper payments in overseas markets provides a dramatic case study of why a corporation with a high-performance, high-integrity culture must just say no.

Notes

Section II

1. The changes in rules that increase board responsibilities include Sarbanes-Oxley legislative provisions, implementing SEC regulations, changes in stock exchange listing requirements, governance requirements imposed by court-ordered monitors in particular cases, and post-Enron corporate rewrites of governance principles and committee charters. Corporate Governance, http://www.corpgov.net/links/links.html, has fourteen pages of links to governance Web sites.

2. From 1995 to 2007, the SEC's budget increased nearly 200 percent, from nearly $300 million to nearly $900 million.

3. Enforcement elsewhere in the developed world is approaching U.S. levels whether it involves privacy or cartel issues in the European Union (EU) or consumer protection in England or Japan. Government inquiries into integrity issues at Parmalat, Shell, Ahold, Volkswagen, and Siemens illustrate the point. Indeed, investigations or controversies in one nation or jurisdiction are now often leveraged by regulators and enforcers in other jurisdictions or nations.

4. Whether particular, existing rules are necessary or framed in the most cost-effective manner is a matter for public-policy debates (see 127–138). But until rules are changed or clarified,

adherence—or avoidance of getting too close to an ambiguous and moving line—is required to avoid significant liability.

5. Constance E. Bagley and Diane W. Savage, *Managers and the Legal Environment: Strategies for the 21st Century* (Mason, OH: Thomson West, 2006), 15. (Directors' state-law duty to manage in "best interests" of corporation does not legally mandate maximizing shareholder value but has generally been interpreted by state courts to allow companies significant latitude in addressing interests of other stakeholders.) See also Einer R. Elhauge, "Corporate Managers' Operational Discretion to Sacrifice Corporate Profits in the Public Interest," in *Environmental Protection and the Social Responsibility of Firms: Perspectives from Law, Economics, and Business*, eds. Bruce L. Hay, Robert N. Stavins, and Richard H. K. Vietor (Washington, DC: RFF Press, 2005), 13–76.

6. E. Merrick Dodd, "For Whom Are Corporate Managers Trustees?" *Harvard Law Review* 45 (1932): 1145, 1154. More than fifty years later, Bill George, former Medtronic CEO, offered the same balanced view: "Trust is everything, because success depends upon customers' trust in the products they buy, employees' trust in their leaders, investors' trust in those who invest for them and the public's trust in capitalism . . . If you do not have integrity, no one will trust you, nor should they." Bill George, *True North: Discover Your Authentic Leadership* (New York: John Wiley & Sons, Inc., 2007), xxv–xxxii.

7. For example, GE has more than 18,000 aircraft engines on more than 8,000 commercial airliners, flying more than 700 million people per year. It has an installed based of nearly 3,000 turbines providing more than 700 gigawatts of capacity——creating one-third of the world's electricity. It has more than 35,000 imaging machines in use around the globe, providing approximately 250 million scans for patients per year. It helps finance tens of millions of consumers and hundreds of thousands of commercial borrowers.

Notes

Section III

1. See generally John P. Kotter and James L. Heskett, *Corporate Culture and Performance* (New York: Free Press, 1992)

2. Accounts of broader BP cultural issues are found in the January 2007 report to the BP board by the independent panel chaired by James Baker ("The Report of the BP U.S. Refineries Independent Safety Review Panel") and in the March, 2007 report of the U.S. Chemical Safety and Hazard Investigation Board ("Investigation Report: BP Refinery Explosion and Fire"); Sheila McNulty, "Blowdown: How Faults at BP Led to One of America's Worst Industrial Disasters," *Financial Times*, December 19, 2006, 17; Ed Crooks, "How Storm Clouds Gathered Over 'Sun King,'" *Financial Times*, January 12, 2007, 9.

   On October 26, 2007, BP entered into a "global" settlement with U.S. authorities to pay fines and penalties totaling $380 million for violations relating to the refinery explosion, oil pipeline leaks/shutdowns, and fraud in energy trading. This included a criminal plea to a felony, and a $50 million fine (the largest ever under the Clean Air Act), for the Texas blast and deaths. Jeremy Grant et al., "BP Hopes $380m Settlement Will Draw a Line Under Scandals," *Financial Times* (London), October 26, 2007, 1.

3. Kenneth Andrews, *Ethics in Practice: Managing the Moral Corporation* (Boston: Harvard Business School Press, 1989).

4. John P. Kotter, "What Leaders Really Do," *Harvard Business Review*, May–June 1990.

5. John P. Kotter, *Leading Change* (Boston: Harvard Business School Press, 1996), 25.

6. There are also important differences across nations and regions. The United States and the EU have different approaches to accounting, competition law, privacy, and tax law that have a significant impact on multinational corporations. Moreover, specialized rules apply to specific product markets: FCC rules for

NBC, FDA rules for GE Healthcare, federal procurement rules for GE engines, and specific emissions rules for GE locomotives or gas turbines. For a summary of the U.S. legal framework for business readers, see Constance E. Bagley and Diane W. Savage, *Managers and the Legal Environment: Strategies for the 21st Century* (Mason, OH: Thomson West, 2006), chapter 1.

7. See, for example, the Ethics Resource Center, http://www.ethics.org/; *Compliance Week*, http://www.complianceweek.com/; and the Ethics & Compliance Officer Association, http://www.theecoa.org/AM/Template.cfm?Section=Home.

8. Other examples include detailed guidelines on controllership, on avoiding improper payments in hiring consultants or distributors in emerging markets, on the proper approach to gifts and entertainment, on specialized training for salespeople in emerging markets, and on required integrity actions for each week of the year in computerized calendars.

9. Other examples include consumer finance leaders having to embed legal and ethical requirements in the highly automated processes for selling (scripts), making credit decisions (nondiscrimination protections), and collecting and monitoring performance (recorded calls). Federal Aviation Administration quality processes and record keeping were integrated into aircraft engine manufacturing. Sourcing leaders were accountable for technical, financial, and ethical issues in qualifying and requalifying suppliers. Business team leaders had responsibility for ensuring that integrity issues were addressed promptly in acquisitions.

10. March 2007 report of the U.S. Chemical Safety and Hazard Investigation Board ("Investigation Report: BP Refinery Explosion and Fire").

11. A basic integrity review has certain distinct elements. First, there is presentation of key metrics. Among the most salient are concerns lodged in the ombuds system, the aging and disposition of private cases filed, formal governmental proceed-

ings (involving a formal subpoena or a filed case), the degree to which compliance processes have been digitized and integrated into business processes, the number of employees receiving training, employee surveys in the business unit, and resources matched to sites and risky markets. Second, risk areas are assessed across several complementary parameters: are process controls strong or developing; should the area be monitored continuously or periodically; does the area deserve immediate attention? Specific risk mitigation plans are presented for high-risk areas. A third area is discussion of significant investigations and cases to understand root causes and needed remediation. Risk assessment and abatement for recent acquisitions is a fourth mandatory subject. Other subjects include close-out reports on issues from the prior review, general emerging market strategies, and descriptions of leadership involvement and communications.

12. Typical areas of concern in recent years were growth outpacing institutional infrastructure, manual accounting in areas where digitization is essential, broken business operating processes (e.g., sales, inventory, production, underwriting), unnecessary organizational complexity, and poorly integrated acquisitions.

13. See, for example, the Organisation for Economic Co-operation and Development (OECD), *Guidelines for Multinational Enterprises*, http://www.oecd.org; and Business for Social Responsibility, http://www.bsr.org/. A good textbook survey from a European perspective is Andrew Crane and Dirk Matten, *Business Ethics: Managing Corporate Citizenship and Sustainability in the Age of Globalization*, 2nd ed. (New York: Oxford University Press, 2007).

14. Lynn Sharp Paine et al., "Up to Code: Does Your Company's Conduct Meet World-Class Standards?" *Harvard Business Review*, December 2005. For one of the most thoughtful and comprehensive analytic discussions of different perspectives on ethics in a business context, see Lynn Sharp Paine, *Value Shift:*

Why Companies Must Merge Social and Financial Imperatives to Achieve Superior Performance (New York: McGraw-Hill, 2003).

15. It is clear that both the Justice Department and the SEC can bring criminal or regulatory proceedings against third party advisors who allegedly aided a corporation that defrauds its investors. But the definitions of the elements of the crime or the regulatory offense are evolving. It was unclear, for several years, whether private shareholders could bring such suits for civil damages, but a recent U.S. Supreme Court case decided that private investors may not sue third party advisors or investment banks unless there was explicit disclosure of their role upon which the investors relied. (*Stoneridge Investment Partners LLC v. Scientific Atlanta Inc.* was argued in October 2007 and decided in January 2008.)

16. Ben W. Heineman Jr., "Caught in the Middle," *Corporate Counsel*, April 2007.

17. In the options backdating investigations, general counsel are just as likely as chief financial officers to be the subject of criminal prosecutions or become defendants in civil cases. In addition to questionable accounting, areas of GC responsibility, such as public disclosure and board processes, are at the core of possible violations.

18. Compare John C. Coffee, *Gatekeepers: The Role of the Professions and Corporate Governance* (New York: Oxford University Press, 2006) (inside staff leaders cannot be independent) with New York City Bar Association, *Report of the Task Force on the Lawyer's Role in Corporate Governance*, November 2006 (inside staff leaders must be independent).

19. ABA Task Force on Corporate Responsibility, "Report of the American Bar Association Task Force on Corporate Responsibility," *Business Law 59* (2003): 145, 157.

20. In a growing number of corporations, the quality of inside lawyers is increasing, and the primary role of providing

broad counseling to business leaders is shifting from law firms to general counsel and corporate legal departments. See Ben W. Heineman Jr., "In the Beginning," *Corporate Counsel*, April 2006 (discussing changes in corporate law departments).

21. These ageless rationalizations are discussed from a manager's perspective in Saul W. Gellerman, "Why 'Good' Managers Make Bad Ethical Choices," *Harvard Business Review*, July 1986.

22. See GE, *Investing in a Sustainable Future: GE 2007 Citizenship Report* (Fairfield, CT: GE, 2007), or http://www.ge.com/company/citizenship; and GE Energy's "Sales Channels University" at http://www.eselearning.com/.

23. Third-party relationships include joint ventures (with controlling or minority shares); sources of supply (first-tier/subtier/equity interests); trading companies or aggregators who do sourcing for the company; and, most difficult of all, distributors, agents, and consultants who stand between the company and the ultimate customer, posing the constant risk of improper payments. For all these relationships, special education and training is necessary for the corporation's employees. For example, in a controlled joint venture, GE required that the entity adopt a performance-with-integrity approach like the parent company's—including comparable education and training. But with a minority stake, the corporation can only ask for, not demand, adoption of such an approach. Most difficult of all is education and training of third-party distributors and agents. The best that can be done may be their acknowledgement that they will follow company integrity policies and a contract term that allows the company to terminate the relationship if policies are violated. (See the discussion of emerging markets, pages 100–111.)

24. Leaders must direct a careful process involving identification of integrity training needs, assessment of necessary resources, careful course development, effective delivery of information, honest assessment of knowledge retention, and continuous reex-

amination of failures, new risks, and new needs—in other words, a classic continuous improvement loop. They also need to see education and training as part of a broader communications strategy involving a range of activities from major speeches to regular discussion at top staff meetings, to inclusion in personnel reviews, to compensation policies.

25. Discussion of the Boeing speech in January 2006 to top company leaders is found at "Boeing's Top Lawyer Spotlights Company's Ethical Lapses," Law Blog, *Wall Street Journal Online*, January 31, 2006, http://blogs.wsj.com/law/2006/01/31/boeings-top-lawyer-rips-into-his-company. GE's own Israel and Japan scandals, where employees failed to come forward and report improper actions, also illustrated in particular business units an impermissible culture of silence for which officers were terminated (see pages 29–34).

26. Under Section 301 of the Sarbanes-Oxley Act of 2002, there is a requirement that a hotline be available for employees and others to report directly to the board of directors or the audit committee any concerns relating to accounting or internal controls (Pub. L. No. 107–204, 116 Stat. 745). At GE, these concerns went simultaneously to the directors and to the ombudsperson—and were investigated by finance and legal staffs like other concerns. As with regular issues in the ombuds system, allegations about people at the top of the company may require, at board direction, an inquiry using outside resources to avoid conflicts of interest. These summary reports indicate important trends: about the businesses, regions, and integrity policies that are the subjects of the reports; about the number of violations; about the time needed to investigate and close out matters; about the level of anonymous reporting; and, as required, about the kinds of systems changes needed as a result of violations.

27. The bottom-up review is also a way for more-senior managers to assess the intensity and commitment of leaders further down in the organization—to gauge employees' sense of

how the business is relating to various regulators. For example, employees at GE's security business will have views on how the business deals with regulators on such issues as compliance with government specs, product safety, employee safety, radiation, testing, labeling, narcotics, and hazardous materials.

28. For example, "Have I determined how new business initiatives (e.g., acquisitions, digitization, or global expansion) change or increase risks relevant to my operation?" Or "Do I identify compliance risks for each of my employees and establish training plans to address those risks?"

Section IV

1. Konstantin Richter, "The House of Siemens," http://www.wsj.online.com/; and Richard Milne, "Siemens Prepares for Its Cultural Revolution," *Financial Times* (London), October 2, 2007 (new CEO "to strip power away from the countries"). Siemens has publicly reported the possibility of $2 billion in improper payments; tax adjustments for improper deductions in the hundreds of millions; and related investigations in a number of nations across the globe in addition to Germany and the United States. David Crawford and Mike Esterl, "Siemens Ruling Details Bribery Across the Globe," *Wall Street Journal*, November 16, 2007.

2. This is measured by business (e.g., GE Aircraft Engines from 2005 to 2007 reduced third parties by more than 50 percent) and by regions (percentage reductions in third parties during a comparable period were, e.g., 22 percent in China, 29 percent in the rest of Southeast Asia, 37 percent in Korea, 10 percent in the Middle East and Africa, and 23 percent in Latin America).

3. James Mulvenon, "Breaching the Great Firewall? Beijing's Internet Censorship Policies and U.S.-China Relations," in *The China Balance Sheet in 2007 and Beyond*, eds. C. Fred Bergsten et al. (Washington, DC: Center for Strategic and International Studies/Peterson Institute for International Economics, 2007).

See also Corey Boles, Don Clark, and Pui-Wing Tam, "Yahoo's Lashing Highlights Risks of China Market," *Wall Street Journal*, November 7, 2007 (Internet firm gives Chinese authorities private data on a user who is ultimately jailed).

4. Joseph Treaster, "Broker Accused of Rigging Bids for Insurance," *New York Times*, October 15, 2004; and Alan Murray, *Revolt in the Boardroom: The New Rules of Power in Corporate America* (New York: Collins, 2007), 47–54.

5. "The Evolving Role of General Counsel: Meeting the Crisis," *National Law Journal*, February 2007 (roundtable discussion, including subsequent MarshMac general counsel, of the causes of and cures for the firm's crisis).

6. See Lynn Sharp Paine, *Value Shift: Why Companies Must Merge Social and Financial Imperatives to Achieve Superior Performance* (New York: McGraw-Hill, 2003). For discussions of delayed reporting in the Ford/Bridgestone, Beech-Nut, and Salomon Brothers controversies. For a quick survey of similar corporate problems during the past thirty years, see Robert Gandossy and Jeffrey Sonnenfeld, eds., *Leadership and Governance from the Inside Out* (New York: John Wiley & Sons, Inc., 2004), xi–xxi.

7. See, for example, Ronald J. Alsop, *The 18 Immutable Laws of Corporate Reputation: Creating, Protecting and Repairing Your Most Valuable Asset* (New York: Wall Street Journal Books, 2004), 222–225.

8. Ten years later, the alleged counterparty, DeBeers Centenary, entered a one-count criminal plea to a conspiracy to restrain trade and paid a $10 million fine. The brief plea agreement did not include any supporting factual details. Owing to antitrust issues dating back to World War II, DeBeers had refused for half a century to have a corporate presence in the United States and submit to the jurisdiction of the U.S. courts. As a result, its officers could not enter the United States, and it had to sell in the United States through intermediaries. According to press reports, De-

Beers had reversed course and decided to establish retail outlets in the United States at the time it entered into the plea agreement. Margaret Webb Pressler, "DeBeers Pleads to Price-Fixing: Firm Pays $10 million; Can Fully Reenter U.S.," *Washington Post*, July 14, 2004. ("Industry experts say the company may have settled because it was too risky to stay away from the U.S. market when so many new sources of diamonds were emerging.")

9. Elizabeth Economy and Kenneth Lieberthal, "Scorched Earth: Will Environmental Risks in China Overwhelm Its Opportunities?" *Harvard Business Review*, June 2007, 92.

10. See Ben W. Heineman Jr., "Hands Across the Water: GE Crafted a 'Foreign Policy' for Doing Business Abroad. Should Your Company Have One Too?" *Corporate Counsel*, October 2006.

11. China is writing laws almost as rapidly as its economy is growing. GE had to develop a computerized legislative tracking system because so many proposals had potential impact on business in such areas as labor, antitrust, taxes, financial leasing, antidumping, intellectual property, energy, and environment. If a business put a high priority on a country issue that was not shared by the country team, corporate leaders would have to reconcile the difference to determine the level of company effort and method of coordinating effort. In China, however, energy and environment were at the top of the list for both GE Energy and China leaders.

12. See, for example, Michael E. Porter and Mark R. Kramer, "Strategy and Society: The Link Between Competitive Advantage and Corporate Social Responsibility," *Harvard Business Review*, December 2006; *Investing in a Sustainable Future: GE 2007 Citizenship Report* (Fairfield, CT: GE, 2007), 7 (Immelt letter).

13. Ibid., *Investing*, 94.

14. Ben W. Heineman Jr. and Fritz Heimann, "The Long War Against Corruption," *Foreign Affairs*, May–June 2006; and Ben W. Heineman Jr. and Fritz Heimann, "Arrested Develop-

ment: The Fight Against International Corporate Bribery," *National Interest*, November–December 2007.

15.   Eric Lipton and Louise Story, "Toy Makers Seek Standards for U.S. Safety," *New York Times*, September 7, 2007; and Eric Lipton and Gardiner Harris, "In Turnaround, Industries Seek U.S. Regulations," *New York Times*, September 16, 2007.

16.   Robert G. Eccles, Scott C. Newquist, and Roland Schatz, "Reputation and Its Risks," *Harvard Business Review*, February 2007, 104. Paul Argenti of Dartmouth's Tuck School is less optimistic about CEO sensitivity: "Why is it so easy for executives to think about and plan for financial risk, but still so hard for them to understand that intangible risks to an organization's reputation are far more likely to destroy shareholder value?" "Special Report: Mastering Risk: The Challenge of Protecting Reputation," *Financial Times* (London), September 30, 2005.

17.   Alsop, *The 18 Immutable Laws of Corporate Reputation*, 11.

18.   The shareholder may care about governance; the creditor about a "fair" balance between growth and stability; the employee about fair wages and conditions or education and training; customers about fair dealing and products with quality and integrity; suppliers about fair standards for qualification and evaluation; local communities about jobs and the environment.

19.   See Porter and Kramer, "Strategy and Society," 81, for a critique of methodologies used by varying entities that rate corporations.

20.   For Web access to the Global Reporting Initiative (GRI), see http://www.globalreporting.org/reportingframwork. GRI principles require reporting companies to present a balance between good and bad; show comparisons over time; and ensure accuracy and reliability (auditors approve facts in report/senior management review). See also Porter and Kramer, "Strategy and Society," 88 (GRI "rapidly becoming a standard for CSR reporting").

21. In mid-2007, GE said that it was selling forty-five technologies that both improved operating performance and significantly and measurably improved the customer's environmental performance under an economic product review conducted by a third-party consultant. See *Investing in a Sustainable Future*, 44–49 (ecomagination discussion). The report also discusses compliance with a 2002 EPA order to dredge PCBs out of the Hudson River (p. 80), GE's most controversial environmental issue. GE had strongly argued against dredging on policy grounds (more environmental harm than good) and had been opposed just as strongly by New York State environmentalists (more environmental good than harm). Although GE did not retreat from this unpopular substantive position, it made sure that it was in procedural compliance with all EPA orders to produce data or submit comments prior to the 2002 decision. And it has been committed to compliance with all procedural and substantive EPA orders since then.

Section V

1. For the importance of a management development process that focuses on traits needed in a CEO, see Joseph L. Bower, *The CEO Within: Why Inside-Outsiders Are the Key to Succession Planning* (Boston: Harvard Business School Press, 2007).

2. See *Agenda: The Week's News from Other Boardrooms*, May 7, 2007 ("Boards tie top executive pay to sustainability goals at Duke, Baxter"), and August 20, 2007 ("Boards tie top executive pay to enterprise risk management objectives"), http://www.AgendaWeek.com/.

3. The most difficult problem arises when there is possible impropriety at the top of the company. If it does not involve the CEO but does involve a direct report or a person close to a direct report, then, hopefully, the CEO, the CFO, and the GC will need

to bring the matter to the board and, usually, recommend an independent inquiry with outside resources to avoid the appearance of a conflict of interest. If the matter does involve the CEO, an independent outside inquiry under board direction is a necessity.

Section VI

1. The productive link between an integrity culture and business process also has a human relations dimension. For example, the nondiscrimination principle is not only important generally in giving all employees a sense of possibility in a global company, but it can help recruit highly talented women who suffer discrimination in, for example, China and Japan. Rather than being in opposition, the emphasis on meeting financial commitments and integrity commitments can be a complementary expression of the core values of honesty, candor, fairness, reliability, and trustworthiness. And a performance-with-integrity culture can be a source of high employee morale, loyalty, and commitment, described above in the discussion of benefits.

2. Finally, some will say that it is fine for a huge company like GE to incur the costs of performance with integrity, but what about the small company? The short answer is, the risks and the benefits are similar. Indeed, the benefits of avoiding risk may be greater in a small company because a major miss can sink the company. Building integrity into business operations as they develop is likely to involve only a fractional cost of the new activity and be a significant investment for the future, especially if the goal is decent but not outstanding systems and processes. Moreover, many small or medium-size companies are hoping for their payday when they are acquired by large companies—but with decent due diligence by the acquirer, the small target will find either that the deal craters because of problems or that there is a significant purchase price reduction. Finally, there is

simply the "look in the mirror" response: what kind of person are you, and what kind of enterprise do you wish to be associated with? It is hard to create a culture of personal values that make companies work—honesty, candor, fairness, reliability, and trustworthiness—when the leadership is indifferent to, or contemptuous of, adherence to formal financial and legal rules and to the establishment of voluntary global standards that respect the important concerns of stakeholders.

To be sure, there will be *scaling* issues in smaller companies. But I believe that the core principles and practices discussed in this book are replicable across companies of all sizes.

Acknowledgments and Dedication

My friends and colleagues at GE taught me so much during my years at the company. I cannot thank them all by name. But obviously, Jack Welch and Jeff Immelt made it all possible—and taught me volumes about what leadership means. Special thanks go to CFOs Dennis Dammerman and Keith Sherin, to HR leader Bill Conaty, to CIO Gary Reiner, to all heads of the corporate audit staff during my tenure (including Charlene Begley, Dave Calhoun, and John Rice), and to all my extraordinary partners in GE Legal, including Zoe Baird, Chris Barecca, Nancy Barton, Frank Blake, Ted Boehm, Raymond Burse, Rick Cotton, Pam Daley, Barbara Daniele, Brackett Denniston, Ugo Draetta, Mark Elborne, Ivan Fong, Mike Gadbaw, Scott Gilbert, Ralph Gonzalez, Kathy Harris, Suzanne Hawkins, Bob Healing, Henry Hubschman, Bruce Hunter, Rick Jackson, Art Joyce, Jeff Kindler, Burt Kloster, Phil Lacovara, Liz Lanier, Jay Lapin, Elizabeth Lee, David Lloyd, Bill Lytton, Steve Maloy, Mike McAlevey, Liam McCollum, Paul McElhiney,

Keith Morgan, Keith Newman, Mark Nordstrom, Happy Perkins, Steve Ramsey, Leon Roday, John Samuels, Bob Sloan, Maura Smith, Peter Solmssen, Nick Spaeth, Ron Stern, and Larry Tu.

I am very grateful for perceptive comments from the following people who read drafts of the manuscript: Joe Bower, Bob Eccles, Ben Heineman Sr., Michael Hershman, Shelly Lazarus, Joshua Margolis, Ken Meyer, Ira Millstein, Joe Nye, Lynn Paine, Bill Perlstein, Gary Sheffer, Bob Swieringa, Noel Tichy, and Sandy Warner. This book grew out of an article in *Harvard Business Review*, and I am deeply appreciative for the guidance from editors Karen Dillon and Ben Gerson. I am especially in debt to Hollis Heimbouch and to Jeff Kehoe of Harvard Business Press for their support and vision, and to Jeff and Jeff Cruikshank for being superb editors.

My wife, Cristine Russell, a brilliant journalist and editor as well as a strong, supportive, and caring person. No words can express my deep reliance on her warmth and wisdom.

. . .

This book is for her, for my sons,
Zach and Matt, and for my parents,
mentors and role models for
more than six decades.

About the Author

Ben W. Heineman Jr. was GE's senior vice president–general counsel from 1987–2003, and then senior vice president for law and public affairs from 2004 until his retirement at the end of 2005. He is currently senior fellow at the Belfer Center for Science and International Affairs at Harvard's Kennedy School of Government and distinguished senior fellow at Harvard Law School's Program on the Legal Profession. A Rhodes Scholar, editor-in-chief of the *Yale Law Journal*, and law clerk to Supreme Court Justice Potter Stewart, Mr. Heineman was also assistant secretary for policy at the Department of Health, Education and Welfare and practiced constitutional law at Sidley Austin prior to his service at GE. He is the author of books on British race relations and the American presidency, and writes frequently on business, law, and international affairs. He is a fellow of the American Academy of Arts and Sciences and serves on the boards of Memorial Sloan Kettering Cancer Center, the Center for Strategic and International Studies, the National Constitution Center, and Transparency International-USA.